Building a Wholesome Family in a Broken World

Also by Eduard Habsburg:

The Habsburg Way: Seven Rules for Turbulent Times

Eduard Habsburg

BUILDING A WHOLESOME FAMILY IN A BROKEN WORLD

Habsburg Lessons from the Centuries

SOPHIA INSTITUTE PRESS
Manchester, New Hampshire

Cover design by Updatefordesign Studio.

Cover photograph courtesy of Eduard Habsburg.

Sophia Institute Press
Box 5284, Manchester, NH 03108
1-800-888-9344
www.SophiaInstitute.com

paperback ISBN 979-8-88911-256-3
ebook ISBN 979-8-88911-257-0

Library of Congress Control Number: 2024944139

First printing

To my wonderful wife, Marie-Theres,
who said yes when I asked her, thirty years ago.
Best decision of our lives!

Contents

Building a Wholesome Family in a Broken World

Introduction

What is a family? A family is the longing of every human being. The family is where life is born, love is first experienced, and faith is first lived. Aristotle described the human being as a *zoon politikon*, or "political animal." But the smallest, most fundamental *polis* (city) is a family. A family is a tiny society, its own miniature world, where the first feelings of friendship and solidarity can flourish. Or as the *Catechism of the Catholic Church* puts it: "The family is the *original cell of social life*. It is the natural society in which husband and wife are called to give themselves in love and in the gift of life" (2207).

It's true, in our age, that many families are broken. But as much as the technocrats in our consumer society would like to keep us all alone, glued to screens and spending money, this is not what we are meant to be. We are meant to be in families—families that are not broken but whole, wholesome, and healthy. Family life is what everybody should be striving for. It is what everybody really wants.

And yet it seems that the family is now more threatened than ever. Young people are struggling to find a partner for life; they don't even know how to start looking. New ideologies and ideologues attack and try to destroy the traditional family, tempting us to redefine and reinvent ourselves whenever we choose, seducing us with the notion that we can be our own gods. Pornography and destructive "dating" sites promise easy pleasure and do their own large part to sow confusion. In such a world, it is not surprising that many people have resigned themselves to isolation and consider family life to be an unattainable dream that now exists primarily in history and novels. (And don't even get me started on divorce rates and dwindling numbers of children.)

What you hold in your hands is a how-to book on forming a happy family, chock-full of nearly a millennium of Habsburg know-how. You will learn about my own experiences of family life: how my wife and I found each other; how we took the plunge and got engaged; how we married and had six beautiful children; how we passed on faith, traditions, and values so our children could start their own families.

But my wife and I did not invent or define these experiences. We learned how to live from our own parents, who had learned from theirs. Our personal experiences will be shown in the context of many beautiful examples from 850 years of my family history. Families are the natural state of human beings. But in Europe, at least, the Casa da Austria, the House of Habsburg, has epitomized family. I will share our story with you.

How did the Habsburgs find the right spouses to create healthy families? Let me say it up front: no, they didn't always marry cousins! But their families did guide them as they grew. How did they bring up their children and teach them the values that families need? How did they pass on their Faith, both when it was easy and when it was hard? You will find out in these pages. And don't worry: my family stories are not dusty, antique tales of imperial intrigue. The Habsburgs' experience with homeschooling is quite instructive for many families today.

In fact, my goal is to show how anyone can start a happy family. You do not need to belong to an ancient one to start your own.

Introduction

Family is possible. Family is beautiful. In fact, next to faith, family is the most important thing in the world. Family is what everyone really wants.

Let me introduce you to mine. I hope, and pray, it will help you with yours.

1

A Brief History of the Habsburg Family

If any European royal family knew about marriage and family, it was the Habsburgs. In fact, there is a Latin saying about the Habsburgs' expertise:

Bella gerant alii, tu felix Austria nube.

May the others wage war, you,
happy Austria, get married.

A family that has been excelling at marriage and family for almost a millennium ought to be able to provide some sound advice. Some of it may have to be translated into our current context. But all of it will be educational, and most of it will be encouraging—though I will give you a few examples of what can happen if you don't do family right.

This book is not primarily about the Habsburgs. It is primarily about how to build a wholesome family today. (Those who want to delve into my family's history, to understand our core principles, and to learn about a few of our more illustrious members should read my first book, *The Habsburg Way*.) But I will provide a very brief overview of our history.

The Habsburg family first rose to historical prominence before the year 1000, in the area around Lake Constance, between what is now Germany, Switzerland, and France. Here they might have remained unremarkable Swiss counts, governing the small area near Habsburg Castle (near Zurich), had not Rudolf von Habsburg been elected king of the Holy Roman Empire in 1273. From that moment until the end of World War I, the Habsburgs helped to shape European—and later world—history.

Their power base began in Austria, but by the 1500s, it had grown to include Hungary and Bohemia, the Netherlands and Belgium, Spain, and finally, large parts of the world. And how was this achieved? To large degree, through well-placed marriages! And some luck.

The now-archducal family then split into two branches for about 150 years, one reigning in Spain and, from there, large parts of the world; the other in Austria and, from there, the Holy Roman Empire. This was a period of frequent interfamily marrying, often between the two branches, which compromised the health of the children (and seems to be a constant source of amusement to certain people). It is also when the famous Habsburg jaw began to appear in paintings.

After 1700, Spain belonged to the French Bourbons, and only the Austrian branch survived. Legendary historical figures, such as Empress Maria Theresia (with her sixteen children) and Emperor Franz Joseph led the Habsburg Empire—now centered in Austria, Hungary, and Central Europe—into the eighteenth, nineteenth, and twentieth centuries. While the Habsburgs were always Catholic, and often devout, it was the last Habsburg emperor, Bl. Karl—who ruled for a brief eighteen months at the end of World War I—who became our family's first "blessed" (and, hopefully one day, saint).

A Brief History of the Habsburg Family

The Habsburg Empire ended with the end of World War I. But the Habsburg family is still going strong. In fact, we have several hundred members who live all over the world—so the sun still never sets on the Habsburgs.[1]

From the beginning, there were certain characteristics that were strongly associated with this special family. Two of the most important were family—with lots of kids—and the Catholic Faith.

Because Habsburg families were staunchly Catholic, they were open to life. Indeed, many had ten or more children, and some as many as eighteen (albeit sometimes with different wives, after the death of the first ones; childbirth was hard).

Divorce was unthinkable.

Mistresses and affairs, which were practically celebrated in other kingdoms, were rare among the Habsburgs. If infidelities did happen, they were handled discreetly and were confessed as sins in the sacrament of Penance.

It goes without saying that the circumstances surrounding archducal marriages were, in important ways, very different from those in our time. Most of us don't live in monarchies, let alone run them. Most of us are not married off to foreign princes or dukes in the interests of political alliances. We typically meet our spouses well before the day of our marriage. Marriage decisions made by parents with little input from their children are uncommon; and no, we are not in the habit of marrying our cousins anymore.

Nevertheless, even if our patterns of courtship are different, the fundamentals of marriage—and the challenges, and joys, of family life—are quite similar. If you are open-minded about history and my family stories, you will learn valuable lessons.

[1] The phrase about the sun never setting on the British Empire was first used about the Habsburg Empire.

Perhaps the most valuable lesson you will learn from this book is the importance of Faith. In fact, family and faith are so intimately intertwined that, before we continue, I wanted to share with you my personal journey of faith so you will know that all of what you will read below is not just dry theory but lived experience.

As you might have gathered from the introduction about my family, I am what is called a "cradle Catholic." I was baptized as a baby and grew up with believing parents who introduced me to the sacraments, to regular prayer, and to the beauty of the Catholic Faith from the earliest days of my life. When I was little, I was encouraged to serve as an altar boy.

My relationship with priests has always been very good. Two brothers of my maternal grandfather were Jesuits, of the old kind: good German Jesuits formed in the 1930s and 1940s with a clear knowledge and gentle love of the Catholic Faith. One of them, Fr. Franz Löwenstein, was my confessor for nearly all of my childhood. I visited his confessional in St. Michael's Church in Munich, Germany, every month as a student, and we often we sat in his room discussing faith, Church history, and the hundreds of questions a budding teenager has about life.

Even closer to home, my brother Paul, who grew up as I did and had nearly all the same influences, has been a priest for decades.

In addition to the personal experiences we had growing up, at that time there was also a gigantic, towering figure on the world stage: John Paul II. He championed our Faith—our identity, in modern terms—and encouraged us to speak about it, to live it, and to rejoice in it. I will never forget his papal visit when we, as youngsters, stood under the windows of the nunciature, late into the evening, hoping we would see him come out—and we did.

From the very beginning of my life, my parents and my grandfather (more about him later) instilled in me a great love for Rome and the papacy—partly by taking me to Rome when I was young and letting me participate in liturgies in St. Peter's. I was also extremely fortunate that my maternal grandfather knew Pope John Paul II, so I had a few personal encounters with him.

From the 1980s on, my family's attendance at daily Mass intensified; we said copious Rosaries; and fasting and a deepening devotion to Our Lady became regular aspects of our lives. These practices have remained with me ever since.

Even so, between the ages of thirteen and eighteen, I struggled with my faith. It was not the dramatic sort of crisis in which you hurl your Bible out the window and become an atheist; those kind of antics are neither in my character nor in my upbringing. But while I continued to go to church and to pray, I did question the existence of God and the reliability of the Gospels. Unfortunately for me, I was living in Germany, and the answers I got there from sad and insecure priests (and the books they gave me to read) did not exactly help. I began to pray less. But I never let go. In fact, I asked God to reach out to me and to let me know that He existed.

And then He did, in a rather personal and spectacular way that I couldn't question. Since then, I have never fallen away or experienced serious doubts again. (I am thankful for that experience, but I think it was less important than the fact that I stuck to my basic prayers.)

When I was older, I received some instruction from Opus Dei for a few years, but I never joined.

When I got married, my wife and I explored charismatic spirituality for a while, but we found that more traditional practices better helped us to grow spiritually. We had a prayer corner of our living room, with an icon and a candle. Rosaries, retreats, and pilgrimages were part of our life. Mostly we were what you call "normal Catholics," active in our parish and teaching our six children the joys of the Faith.

Since I became an ambassador in Rome, my wife and I have discovered the Traditional Latin Mass. It has continued to shape our lives ever since. I would have never expected that after an entire life devoted to other forms of Catholic prayer, an "old dog" like me could learn a new trick. But I did. And it has invigorated our common faith. That doesn't mean I don't regularly go to the modern Mass too. But the Latin Mass has transformed me. Before we began attending the Latin Mass, we prayed the Rosary only when we felt moved to do so; now we pray it daily—and our children, thanks be to God, pray it too. In fact, all of our kids are, thanks again to God, on a good faith path, and that is an incredible gift.

So you see, over the years, my Faith has been the cornerstone of my life, my marriage, and my family—and in many forms. I've learned that, whether you sing along with the guitar or kneel and mutter your prayers in Latin, as long the practice is in accordance with the Catholic truth and brings you closer to holiness and deepens your relationship with God, it is to be welcomed. As the old prayer beseeches, "Sancta Maria, Mater Dei, ora pro nobis peccatoribus, nunc et in hora mortis nostrae." Or, as the contemporary song "A Place in the Choir" has it: "All God's critters got a place in the choir / Some sing low, some sing higher." So rejoice in your Faith always. And with that in mind, let us turn to how to find a spouse, get married, start a family—and all the rest!

2

Courtship and Finding the Right Spouse

A word of warning at the beginning: to some readers, the advice that I am going to give may seem old-fashioned or even reactionary or impossible to follow. While this advice may find favor in large parts of the United States, it will likely cause indignation, even anger, in most of Europe. But consider that what I am about to describe has been the normal way of life throughout recorded history. It is only in the last few decades that what I am recommending has fallen out of favor in our society.

Okay, here we go.

Chastity

We have an old saying in my family: if you are not faithful to your future wife *before* you marry her, you won't be faithful to her *after* you have married her. More broadly, if you want a durable, happy, fulfilling marriage, and if you want to find the right "significant other," you've got to do things right from the beginning—and I mean the very beginning. Your preparation for marriage has to begin *years before you actually date the girl or guy of your dreams.*

What does this mean? Let me be blunt: I firmly believe that with every premarital relationship, started and broken off, you lessen your chances of having a lifelong, happy, fulfilling marriage and life. That may sound very strange to many modern ears—and it doesn't mean that it is impossible to create a happy marriage after a long string of relationships. With enough work, prayer, and grace, anything is possible. But your odds are best if you are faithful to your spouse *before* you even get to know him or her.

What I am talking about is the old and much-maligned word *chastity*. Chastity is the way to happiness.

In the Western world today, for most children, sexuality is aggressively introduced in school. Whether through pornography on a school friend's cell phone, or on their own phone, or in state-mandated "health" class—the schools are now graphic with respect to technique and silent with respect to everything else—sexuality is not introduced as the expression of a trusting, loving, lifelong relationship between one man and one woman. Rather, kids are pressured to embark early upon sexual adventures, avoiding only two dreaded consequences: catching a disease and getting pregnant.

The message that is transmitted is that it is quite normal to begin sexual relationships in one's teens; indeed, those who don't do so are considered weird. Girls especially are made to feel awkward and "not with it" if they don't follow the crowd. The conventional wisdom encourages people to have quite a few relationships before they "settle down," to have some "fun" before life gets "boring."

And so you young people might embark on a parade of relationships. And every time you develop an intimate bond with someone and later chop it off, it makes you more unhappy and less able, ultimately, to enter into a serious and durable relationship.

Young men who learn early on that they can have the girls they want without any responsibility are understandably unwilling to commit to long-term relationships. But worse are the parents who stand by, smiling and muttering something like "Well, they are young; they must have some fun. I was young too once."

This attitude makes me extremely angry. Marriage, in this context, is seen as some ceremony of little import that supplements a relationship, often because the woman wants to have an occasion to wear a white dress and have a celebration. But the relationship has already been built on an unstable foundation. Even if the couple has a house together—or even children—the relationship is simply an expression of their mutual desire to be together. It is not surprising that the little marriage ceremony fails to do much more to hold these relationships together. There is so little behind the marriage beyond a bit of musty tradition.

But what about it? Some will say that's "just the way it is today," right? Well, it doesn't have to be.

It wasn't the case for me or my wife. It certainly wasn't the case for all those couples I know who have had long, happy, deeply fulfilling, joyful marriages. It wasn't the case for centuries. In fact, until very recently, it was never the case.

Some may ask: In a time of omnipresent pornography, strings of uncommitted relationships, and sex without any responsibility, how could anybody live in a totally different way? The sexual revolution of the 1960s and contraception have changed the world forever.

Perhaps. But the sexual revolution has created an awful lot of misery. And you don't have to live that way. You really don't.

Let me propose something highly countercultural and revolutionary: I want you to make a great plan for your future family life. I want you to take a great gamble and give up a few experiences for a few years. I want you to sacrifice a little bit of "fun" for the chance to win lifelong happiness.

Never believe the lies of those who tell you that a lifelong love with one spouse will be dull, drab, or boring. It is the greatest thing I know in the world.

Habsburg Models of a Chaste Life

For most Habsburgs, it was absolutely unthinkable to live together before marriage. The reason for this was partly geographical: future spouses often lived several countries apart. But the Habsburgs also knew, through their Faith, that sexuality belongs in marriage and must be open to life. (The very first commandment in the Bible is "Be fruitful and multiply" [Gen. 1:22].) While chastity may seem an unreachable ideal today, it is the rampant and unrestrained promiscuity of our times that is the historical aberration. After all, being unchaste was just as much a temptation in the days of the Habsburg Empire. Can you imagine how easy it would have been for an archduke, or a future emperor, to find lovers?

I am not saying they never sinned; we are all sinners, after all. Indeed, some of their transgressions are well known. For instance, the great Don Juan of Austria, who won the battle of Lepanto, was an illegitimate child of Charles V. Still, there was a clear recognition of the wrongness of the act and the desire for forgiveness through Confession—and Charles later legally recognized Juan as his son.

But though some Habsburgs stumbled, many did not—and their marriages show the value of chastity. Emperor Ferdinand I (1503–1564) was the brother of Charles V. His biographers attest that he was a chaste youth and married as a virgin. His wife saw their marriage first and foremost as a sacrament; and their relationship with each other was described as especially tender and close. Three of his daughters later discerned a vocation to the monastery, among them Ven. Magdalena of Austria.

As a side note, it is perhaps worth mentioning that this was at almost the same time that the English King Henry VIII's complete lack of chastity led him to marry six times and break the Church of England off from the Catholic Church. The consequence of his lack of self-control was centuries of Catholic persecution, and the brutal martyrdom of hundreds of Catholics, among them many priests. (It was not without reason that Ferdinand I was appalled by Henry VIII.)

Ferdinand's grandson, Emperor Ferdinand II, who ruled during the Thirty Years' War, was a deeply devout Catholic and was well known for his chaste life before marriage. He didn't tolerate even immoral talk or behavior around him. When a servant tried to talk him into a "gallant adventure," he immediately fired him.

Again, to help explain these men, it is worth noting that both Ferdinand I and Ferdinand II began each day with prayer and Holy Mass. This is very important: living the Catholic Faith fully helps one to live a chaste life.

When Empress Maria Theresia fell in love with Franz Stephan (Francis of Lorraine), she was, of course, never allowed to meet him alone. After their engagement in 1735 and until their marriage, he wasn't even allowed to live in the same city as she did. He moved to Bratislava to avoid temptations and scandal.

Archduke Charles, the heroic general who was the first man to beat Napoleon in a land battle, was renowned for his fidelity to his wife. He said in a letter that his marriage was undertaken "to give my unspoiled heart its rights." His marriage was long and very happy.

In some ways, Bl. Emperor Karl, the last Habsburg emperor, was very similar to Ferdinand II. His Faith shaped his decisions as an emperor. But he was also a pure and chaste young man and never had affairs; when he got married in 1911, his wife was the first and only woman he ever loved. Like Ferdinand II, he didn't tolerate lascivious talk when he was a soldier in the army and always cut such conversations off.

Of course, Emperor Karl's attitude was the fruit of a deep and lived Catholic Faith, and that explains why his behavior was so different from that of other archdukes in those decades. (Indeed, his own father, Archduke Otto, lived a terribly unruly and unchaste life.)

All of these marriages were happy, fulfilling, and blessed with many children—which, alas, is not the case with so many marriages contracted on modern terms. But one example I want to put particularly before your eyes is that of Maria Theresia, who had a decades-long, very happy marriage, with *sixteen children*. She loved her husband, passionately, until his death. After he died, she never married again, and when she herself died, a sheet of paper that noted how long her happiness with Franz Stephan had lasted was found in her prayer book. It is so wonderfully edifying that I want to share it with you:

> 29 years, 6 months, 6 days; at the same hour I took his hand, also on a Sunday, he was suddenly taken from me. Makes together: Years, 29, months, 335, weeks, 1540, days 10.781, hours 258.744.

Lest you think that theirs was a sober and dutiful marriage, here's an example of how Franz Stephan and Maria Theresia spent Shrove Tuesday 1743, after *seven years of marriage* and *six children*: they celebrated the last night before Lent in Möllersdorf Castle, then attended a ball in Vienna on the Neuer Markt, wearing domino masks, danced until eight o'clock in the morning (which was the custom in those days), and finally, changed their outfits and participated in the Ash Wednesday ceremonies at nine o'clock in the morning.

And did I mention that the couple had *sixteen children* over twenty years of marriage?

Theirs was the kind of all-embracing, life-fulfilling marriage that is possible if you commit yourself fully and faithfully to it—from the very beginning.

Let me give you another example. Here are some excerpts from a few letters that Maria Theresia's chaste grandson, Archduke Charles, wrote to his wife, Henriette, after years of marriage and six children:

> When away from you I feel even more how I am tied to you. There are very few men as happy as I, I believe.
>
> Much happiness in this world and in the Beyond may Heaven grant you for all the good you do to me.
>
> Although you know it well, and have heard it often from me, I need first and foremost to repeat to you how deeply and tenderly I love you.

Not bad, right? These are the sorts of things most spouses would sigh to be told. And here's what Bl. Karl said on his deathbed to his wife, Zita, after eleven years of marriage and eight kids: "I love you endlessly."

I repeat: Isn't this the kind of marriage you want? Wouldn't you make sacrifices to have it? Remember, these are the feelings of people who had been *chaste* before and during their marriages.

The Habsburg examples teach us something else: the chastity of these "imperial singles" did not stem from some strange cult of virginity (though undoubtedly they wanted to avoid having children before marriage). Rather, it was an expression of a lived Catholic Faith that warned that having intimate relationships before marriage is a deadly sin and a threat to eternal salvation. The temptation of lust is powerful. It requires spiritual strength to resist it. I strongly believe that to live a chaste lifestyle requires that you have a strong faith life as well. But you must learn your Faith before you can live it: Habsburg parents instilled the Faith in their children's heads at a very tender age and taught them well about the meaning of life, love, and marriage.

Indeed, these lessons should be learned early in life, before young adults ever enter the chaotic and frenzied arena of contemporary dating and marriage. Parents bear a terrible responsibility: if children are abandoned to the influence of school administrators and the pressures of peer groups—or worse, if parents themselves encourage their children to have boyfriends or girlfriends prematurely—those parents are not only pointing them down the path of unhappiness but are endangering their souls. And if parents are reluctant to parent their children because they don't want conflict with them or they want to be their children's best friend, they are not fulfilling their duty.

Parents should not just shrug and parrot the old cliché "That's just the way it is today." They should try harder. Their children are . . . their children! Parents owe this to their children.

Now, here's something very specific parents can do for their children: before their children become teenagers—ideally, long before—parents can encourage them to *pray every day in their evening prayers for their future spouse*. I did this when I was young. My wife did the same. I am sure our marriage is so happy because of it.

Faith

Whatever confusion muddles certain modern minds, it is obvious to most people that men and women are incredibly different. They are different physically. They have different joys and sorrows. They tend to have different interests and circles of friends.

Of course, every human being is a little different from every other. God's gift of love and attraction brings us together. But if you are forming a lifelong relationship, in addition to love and attraction, it is exceedingly helpful to have a common faith. Indeed, let me lay my cards on the table: I think your best chance for a happy marriage and a happy life is to marry a devout Catholic—and even more important, to be, or become, Catholic yourself.

This should not surprise you. I am Catholic, and I believe in my Faith. It would be much stranger if I were Catholic and I didn't think Catholicism—and its teachings on love, marriage, and sexuality—had the truest understanding of what makes for a successful lifelong relationship between one man and one woman. I believe that if you give God a voice in your marriage, He will help you and your spouse to love and respect each other and to grow ever closer to each other.

Of course I believe this.

Having said that, if you believe that another belief system will give you the same support in your non-Catholic denomination or your non-Christian faith, I pray that God blesses your path! And if you don't believe in any higher being but believe that you are still able to have a deep, lifelong, meaningful marriage with fidelity and respect, good luck.

But again, I believe that the Catholic Faith is true; that it leads to lifelong happiness; and that its prayers and rituals—and its saints—will help you to survive when life is unhappy. (I also know that the Habsburgs have always been Catholic. That must count for something.)

Since a shared faith—ideally, a shared Catholic Faith—is at the top of my list of what to look for in a spouse, I should add a disclaimer before continuing: *always* keep an open mind and consider whether God wants you in a different vocation, a religious vocation. My brother is a priest; my wife's brother is a priest; two of my grandfather's brothers were priests, and two of his sisters had vocations to the convent.

All of these men and women had a profound influence on many of my siblings and cousins; in fact, my family would not look the way it does today if these people had not said yes, "Here I am, Lord," to God's call.

In fact, one of them, the devout Sophie zu Eltz, was married, but after her husband died in an accident, and after her children were grown, she entered a convent. As she was discerning her vocation—and after she took her vows—she wrote wonderful, funny, exciting stories about the saints who are honored in the different seasons of the Church year. These stories were published as books in Germany and helped generations of children grow in their Faith. Every year, my mother read me the Advent book, titled *Unter dem Adventskranz* (Under the Advent wreath). I read it to my children. My children already have copies to read to theirs.

Sophie zu Eltz, through her *two* vocations—as a mother and then as a nun (and a writer)—really changed the world. So remember, desiring a family and wishing for a person to love you does not exclude a religious vocation any more than difficulty finding a spouse indicates that you have a religious vocation. Life is complicated. But I encourage you, as you embark on the search for someone to give your life to, to consider that it may be God Himself.

The List

A shared faith is the first thing you should look for in a spouse, but there are a few other things that I think are very important. Here is my list:

1. A shared Faith, ideally Catholic
2. The same idea of family and openness to children as a priority in life
3. A shared idea of chastity and modesty and a generally upright character
4. A certain complementarity of personality
5. A similar cultural background, which tends to make things simpler, though differences are surmountable if points 1 through 4 are met

Perhaps you noticed that I didn't include "attractive," "sexy," or "hot" in that list. I did this deliberately for three reasons. First, these elements will naturally play their roles anyway. You yourself will know best whether, and how, they apply.

Second, these superficial characteristics can, and will, change over time. Life and health take their toll, and there will always be people younger, hotter, and perhaps more physically attractive than your spouse. It is not your spouse's beauty that will carry you through the decades of life's adventures. It is your spouse's heart and soul, faith, and disposition of character. If an accident confines one of you to bed for six months and leaves you helpless, it won't be the other's good looks that does the spoon-feeding. Beauty matters only so much when your baby is crying at three in the morning, teething—and has been for the last two weeks. And don't be frightened by the tougher parts of married life. Just realize that if you have to choose between beauty and a good heart, it's an easy choice. (Ideally you will find both!)

Third, I think that attraction grows with knowledge, respect, and a common experience. I am far more in love with my wife now than when I met her and got engaged. A woman needn't be Helen of Troy to be the right woman—and anyway, look at what happened to Helen.

Falling in Love

"Yes, Archduke, but what about falling in love? Doesn't that play a role? Are you against dancing and flirting and romance? I hope you're not a Puritan (gasp!) who can conceive only of marriages of pure reason."

Sigh. Of course not.

You can't help falling in love! Most people fall in love a lot, and it's a beautiful thing. By all means, go out, go to parties, dance, even flirt. This is fun and a natural part of human life. Just keep in mind that while falling in love *can* be an indication that you have found Mr. or Mrs. (or Archduchess) Right, it doesn't have to be. Just ask your married friends how often they fell in love and how many people they married.

What I do suggest is that before you take a relationship in a serious direction, you step back, take a deep breath, and recheck the checklist. It may provide a perspective that is more reliable and objective than your impassioned feelings.

"Dating"

If you and someone else begin to get serious about each other, you will want to spend lots of time together. You will feel, of course, the wonderful feeling of getting to know each other. (I'm a Catholic, not a Puritan—see above.) But don't stop thinking. Find out whether your ideas and interests are compatible, whether your personalities are complementary, whether you click. Learn about the other person's background, family, and history.

But do not have an intimate relationship with each other. Not at this point.

Don't. Just don't.

Definitely don't.

Why? It is hard enough to be rational when you are dreamily in love; hard enough to judge, impartially, whether it can work out—forever. It is impossible to think clearly about your future when you are thinking about physical passion. You have years—decades and decades, I hope—for all that.

"But don't I have to test whether we are physically compatible?" you ask.

What silliness! You have the argument inside out and backward and upside down. If you are right for each other, and if you love each other, and if you are made for each other, you will grow together and live together and love together—and you will be very "physically compatible." It stands to reason.

If people give you a puzzled look because, as a discerning couple, you will not take a room together when traveling, have faith and remember that you are working courageously to build a wholesome family in an unwholesome world. If the world has gone mad, don't be afraid to do something that the world considers madness.

But now let us go through the checklist in more detail.

Why Faith?

I mentioned faith above as the first, best, and most important thing to look for in a spouse. But now I want to tell you more about why. We are all poor sinners, and marriage is a great undertaking. Temptations, especially with respect to purity and fidelity, are everywhere—to a degree never before seen, I think. If you are a devout Catholic, you can pray for strength; you can regularly carry your faults to Confession and confront them; you also live in constant awareness that you will live your marriage before God. These gifts give you a much better chance for your great undertaking to succeed.

Faith can also help you to discern whether the two of you should embark on the "great journey" together in the first place. How? You can pray together. And you should.

Mother Teresa was fond of quoting Fr. Patrick Peyton's famous phrase "The family that prays together stays together." The same goes for couples. You improve your chances of building a solid relationship—or discovering whether it is really good—if you pray together while you are getting to know each other. I know of couples who prayed the Rosary together, in person or over the phone, long before they got engaged. It is good to welcome God into your discernment process from the beginning. It is also good training for the time that you will live together, if you end up together.

We live in crazy, chaotic times. You and your spouse have no idea how your decades of life together will unfold. You may have wonderful times of abundance; you may live in times of war or famine; you may have many children or none; you may be healthy, or one—or both—of you may be bedridden for years. You have no idea. Putting God in the center of your life will give you the best chance of handling whatever comes your way, particularly with the help of the Catholic Church.

Is having a devout spouse a perfect, money-back guarantee that your marriage will succeed? Alas, no. We are all poor, broken sinners who are free—and prone—to make mistakes, to hurt other people, to behave in innumerable stupid and selfish ways. Even in devout marriages, there can be crises and sometimes ruptures.

But even then, faith will give you the hope and the strength to get up again and hobble your way forward.

Ideas about Family

When considering someone for a spouse, talk a lot about what you expect from your future family life. After all, your potential future spouse may have had very different experiences; he or she—or maybe you—might want only one or two children or might not want to have children at all. Maybe one of you thinks children will interfere with a career or with future education or will be expensive—all very reasonable things to discuss. Talk about whether you are open to life. Often people have never met anybody who advocates having many children or have thought much about it themselves. As a Habsburg and a Catholic—and as someone who has experienced the spectacular joy of a large family—I always advocate having many children. (As a certain Mandalorian says, "This is the way.") But the desire for a large family is met with absolute astonishment in a world where one and a half children, but two cars, is seen as the summum bonum, the greatest good.

The Catholic teaching (and the right way) is that sexuality should be open to life. If your potential spouse is not open to having children—or has a heart that is open enough for only one and a half children—seriously consider looking for somebody else. A Catholic marriage should be open to children. Full stop. So, before you tie the knot, be sure to find out where your potential spouse stands on welcoming children. Marriage is forever.

Try also to get to know a potential spouse's family, to understand more about the realities that person grew up with. Is she a child of divorce? Does he always fight with his younger brother? Does she have siblings, or is she an only child who always dreamt of a big family? All of this is helpful while discerning.

If family is a very important element in your prospective spouse's life—something that will take precedence, something he or she will make sacrifices for—that is a very good sign. People sometimes grow in faith. But pray hard to find out if you should really try to build a future with someone whose faith is tepid.

And be honest with yourself. Don't think: "I will change him [or her] later on." Through grace and the wonderful experience of love in marriage, people can become better versions of who they already are. But most people change very little. With most people, what you see is what you'll get. So be sure it is what you want—and what God wants for you.

Why Chastity?

We discussed chastity above. But like faith, chastity is so important that it must be discussed in depth. Chastity, as I understand it, does not mean "no sex" but rather "sex where it belongs"—in a stable, lifelong marriage of mutual respect that will allow both partners to grow and flourish; and of course, in a marriage open to children.

Again, it is very difficult to lead a chaste and chivalrous life nowadays. Remember, in order to be chaste in marriage, you must work on chastity before your marriage, not only by refraining from intimacy but also by protecting yourself from corrupting influences such as pornography.

Chastity will sharpen your ability to see another individual as a *person*, with his or her own needs and boundaries, and not as an object to be used to satisfy or gratify oneself, as contemporary culture would have it.

Here's an old joke. Two friends meet after not having seen each other for some time. One of them says: "It may surprise you to learn that I have just taken a vow of chastity, obedience, and poverty." The other one says mischievously: "Oh, did you just get married?"

But seriously, marriage without chastity is simply impossible. Find a partner who understands this.

I know it is not easy, particularly these days. For one thing, the people who have the right attitude about chastity are often uncomfortable talking about it—and rightly so. Part of chastity is a certain bashfulness when it comes to intimate matters. But you should try to have a meeting of the minds about this matter before you enter into a marriage. (And if you have been unchaste, it would be a good idea to get "old ties" and past relationships out of the way by confessing these too.)

Complementarity of Personalities

It hardly needs saying, but you must have a complementarity of personalities to make a good marriage. However, unlike physical attraction—which really does take care of itself (sometimes at first sight)—you do need to spend time with each other to know whether you vibe, whether you click, whether you have enough in common (and even whether you have enough differences) to have a good balance. You need to learn about your respective upbringings. If your "worlds" are too different, it may be difficult to handle the challenges that you will face in everyday life. And remember: your next decades together will consist, mostly, of a lot of everyday life.

A good discernment tool is whether, when you are together, you are basically at peace. That doesn't mean complete emotional harmony or some mystical synchronization—you have just barely met. But if the other person is good for you, and if God wants you two together, you should both feel as if "we understand each other," that "it is good when we are together."

Do you see now why it is madness to have an intimate relationship at this point? Physical intimacy pours an emotional balm over everything and smooths all the little points of friction, the disagreements, the differences. This is partly why it helps bond marriages together. But before you are married, your senses will tell you, "We are good together," even if you might not be—not for a lifelong commitment.

Can you laugh with each other? There is no one I can laugh with as well as my wife, but that is also the wonderful result of a long marriage. I don't mean that you must have *exactly the same sense of humor.* Some people love long jokes; some like pithy ones or puns—or even dad jokes! But if you can laugh together, you will find that laughter is one of the most powerful weapons against the vicissitudes of life.

Life and love and laughter are not exact sciences. In none of this will you have absolute, definitive certitude. But take a hard look at these things before you vow your lives to each other.

Since you are not having an intimate relationship—right? right?—your mind should not be too clouded by the attractiveness of the other person to think clearly.

Cultural Background

Love may be the greatest mystery in the world. But life can be surprisingly practical. You do need to consider some practical matters with respect to your potential spouse. Suppose you are a city girl and he lives in a dark mansion on a lonely island in the Outer Hebrides with no neighbors at all. He may be handsome and devout, but can you—should you—give up all of your friends and move there, potentially for the rest of your life?

She seems the perfect match. But what if she is tied to her mother, or studies ice floes in Antarctica all winter, or is committed to caring for her handicapped sister, potentially for years? Should you marry her?

Perhaps. In fact, I think that if the rest of my list checks out, such practical matters should probably not keep you from marrying the person. But do take a hard, realistic look at yourself. There are some factors that make marriage very, very hard. (What if he is manic-depressive—or just has a depressive personality?) Marriage is forever, and forever is a long time.

One suggestion: consider the opinion of your family. Ask your parents and siblings about your potential spouse. While their judgment may not be perfect, neither is yours. And your closest family members usually know you very well and often have more than a vague idea about what would do you good. I know that some people have difficult relations with their families. But if your parents and siblings *all* strongly warn you about somebody, you should take their concerns seriously.

What If You Don't Find a Spouse?

I know of many young men and women who would love to find a good spouse but have had only bad experiences. Some have given up looking. This book has been written partly for you.

First, never lose hope. Pray, pray, pray, and ask God to show you the path to your future spouse. Oh, and did I mention becoming a Catholic makes things *much* easier? I might have.

But also be sober and strategic. It is possible that your future devout, chaste, family-loving, stunning spouse is living just across the street and will one day ring your doorbell to borrow some flour. But don't count on it; this is an unwholesome world. You may have to cast your net a little wider.

There are plenty of good, devout people who are looking for a husband or a wife, and not a few of them are easy on the eye. In fact, I am asked regularly—often by sweet, pretty girls and kind, handsome guys—"How do I find a spouse as good as Bl. Karl or Zita?" So there is definitely hope.

The Habsburgs had their own challenges when it came to finding compatible spouses. They may have been different from modern concerns. Among other things, they had to worry about the state as well as their own happiness. So how did they find spouses? They knew where to look. They married only other Catholics, and ideally from other courts in Europe where they could be sure that the future spouses had the same principles, the same devotions, and the same basic ideas about family.

When you're hunting buffalo, you go to a watering hole, not the woods. When you're looking for a "devout Catholic spouse," you probably shouldn't begin in a bar. Devout Catholics are found, first of all, congregating around parishes and churches.

If your own parish is populated primarily by elderly, well-meaning ladies, consider scouting out other parishes in your town—or even farther away. Monasteries, retreats, local or national pilgrimages, and youth encounters bring together droves of devout Catholics. In fact, conferences on Bl. Karl are perfect opportunities, as they attract precisely the kinds of people who share your principles. (There's an annual Bl. Karl conference in Dallas that has a side program for singles looking for spouses.)

Or visit your cousin in Iowa because she told you there are "very nice, good young men" in her parish. Or your aunt in California. Know that there are many others who are in this game, and that your opportunities in these milieus may be better than those at home.

If you think that this is all insufficiently romantic (and too full of hunting motifs), you are always free to stalk the mysterious, martini-toting beauty at the party you are attending. Who knows? Maybe the person is a good, devout Catholic. Maybe.

Also, don't overlook Catholic dating sites. That may sound even less romantic than hunting. But there are hundreds of happy marriages that have come about because people exchanged parameters online and found a partner for life. I know one couple who found each other on different continents and who now are happily married, with several children.

Think about it. Many Habsburg princes and princesses over the centuries found their spouses in a way not so different from meeting someone through a modern dating site (although the matching was done by their parents). They saw a picture, prayed it was lifelike (and not Photoshop-enhanced), wrote each other courteous letters, and then got married.

So don't lose hope! Your spouse may be waiting for you on another continent.

Finally, you might consider a pilgrimage to a sanctuary of Bl. Karl or begin a novena to this humble giant of faith and family life. Never forget to pray.

3

Getting Engaged and Getting Married

Taking the Plunge

You've found each other! You've spent time together and mapped the interior landscape of your soulmate. You've also listened to the voice of your heart. You have examined my list and checked it twice. And you haven't let your judgment be clouded by too much emotional—or physical—interference.

When is the right moment to jump in and get engaged?

We live in a time when the most difficult thing seems to be making any commitment, to say nothing of a permanent promise that will bind for the whole of life. It is no surprise that some people hesitate endlessly, even if they both know they are right for each other.

Why do they hold back? For three reasons.

First, they are afraid to give up their freedom—even when this fabled freedom, the main idol of our day, is the source of so much modern unhappiness. Second, however well suited they are for each other—and even when nearly all the boxes are checked—they believe that they may still find "a better deal." We live in a consumerist, perfectionist society in which dating apps and swiping apps create such an illusion of options that it seems foolish to settle for only one. Third, because they expect complete fulfillment in another person, only a dream prince or a fantasy princess who caters to their every wish will do. This nineteenth-century idea of romantic love permeates the pages of romance novels. But love is not a steamy feeling; it is an act of giving and a commitment of self.

Feelings and Decisions

We have been living in a dictatorship of feelings for the last two hundred years. But it has become especially tyrannical in the last twenty. In fact, we have been told so often throughout our lives that everything should be governed by our feelings that we forget about our minds.

I want to make this point very clear. In fact, I want you to write this down—literally. Get a pen and a piece of paper and write this:

Love, like faith, is ultimately a decision.

I want to repeat this: Love, like faith, is ultimately a decision.

"Wait a minute, Archduke. Did I hear you right? How can faith be a decision? If there is anything that is built on feelings, it is faith, right? How could I decide to become Catholic, for example, if I don't feel that I have a loving relationship with the invisible God? If I don't feel comforted by Him? If I don't feel at home at Holy Mass? How can faith not be about how I feel?"

Because faith is about truth, and it is our minds that perceive what is true. Yes, they are informed by our hearts. Feelings do matter. They can tell you a lot. But they can be fickle too. It is our minds that know what is true.

"But isn't love, at least, all about feelings? Love can't really be a decision, can it?"

My mother, a very wise woman, always told me: your religious feelings—like your current feelings for your spouse—might depend on the amount of coffee you have had that morning. And yet we are constantly told today that feelings are the one thing we can rely on! I have feelings for someone. So I move in with him. Then those feelings are gone. So I move out.

If I enjoy Holy Mass, if my prayers are full of feeling, if I feel loved, then I am a good and faithful Catholic. If I have periods of spiritual dryness in my prayer life, if I have doubts about God, if my prayers aren't immediately answered in the way I expect … *hasta la vista*? I am an atheist now?

You see how silly that all is.

If you have discerned that something is right, or that something is true, you should put your trust in it. In fact, if you follow the truth, your feelings will follow you.

Habsburg Engagements

Habsburg engagements, like Habsburg courtships, were often arranged by parents. But remember, this was how marriage was arranged in most societies, for many people, for much of history. Nowadays, we take it for granted that we should freely marry whomever we choose. But are modern marriages so obviously more successful than historical ones? Many, many Habsburg marriages were happy, while many modern marriages go catastrophically wrong. Why?

For one thing, parents were not monsters. Ferdinand I, who had fifteen children, did engage in marriage politics. But he always made sure that the spouses he chose for his children were devout; he invested a lot of time in figuring out whether their characters were complementary. And he allowed three of his daughters to pursue spiritual vocations. (He could have married them off for political reasons.)

Am I suggesting managing engagements, as the Habsburgs did in the past? Nope.

But there are good lessons to be learned. If your courtship is informed by a set of rules, your engagement should be informed by them as well. When you know that things are right, jump. You probably won't get the throne of Naples or France as part of the deal. But you may get lifelong happiness.

The Decision

You've freely chosen your spouse. Good. But now your decision to love—like a decision of faith—must be repeated, freely, for the rest of your life. Remember all those minutes, hours, days, months, and years that Maria Theresia jotted down on her paper? It is not just the first moments that matter, but all of them.

And here we have come full circle once again. Many people hesitate to get engaged because they still don't feel that all of their feelings are right. But most people are feeling their way in the dark. Of course you feel funny. You are thinking about spending the rest of your life with someone. That should feel different from anything you've ever felt before.

You see, in the end, you will *never* have enough information to make a qualified decision. You will never be ready. You will never have 100 percent certainty. You are going to promise to stand by your spouse in good times and in bad, in sickness and in health—and nobody ever has enough information to justify, rationally, such a jump.

But that is why a list like mine can be such a great help. If most of the points on my list are satisfied, you will know that you are basing your decision on rational foundations.

So relax. Pray. Decide. Jump.

How I Got Engaged

Let me tell you how I knew that the right moment for my engagement had come. Though I had never set down my principles in writing, as I have done here, I had always known them instinctively and tried to live accordingly. For instance, I never dated a woman whom I could not imagine marrying, even if I might have fallen in love with her.

But when I realized how taken I was with my future wife, and when I had the impression that the attraction was mutual, after many conversations we began to pray a novena together. It was a novena to the Holy Spirit, from an old prayer book. One line from it struck me and stuck with me:

Vom Widerstand gegen die erkannte Wahrheit—
befreie uns, o Herr.

From resistance to the known truth—
deliver us, O Lord.

Shortly thereafter, my future wife and I went on a pilgrimage to a Marian shrine together. Once again, we were immersed in one of our long conversations, this time at the foot of a cross beside a church. I had the impression that we both knew, and had known for a while, that it was the right thing to do. But someone had to make a move. Suddenly I remembered that line from the prayer, and I thought, "How much clearer can it get?" So without a ring, without any planning, and without all of the romantic accoutrement this moment is supposed to require, I asked her.

And she said yes.

It was the best decision of my life, our life.

We got engaged because of those words: "From resistance to the known truth—deliver us, O Lord."

From the moment I met my future wife for the first time (at a wedding, which I will tell you more about later) to the moment we got engaged was a frighteningly short eight weeks. Nine months later, we were married. I don't suggest this breakneck speed for everybody. But here we are, thirty years and six children later, very happily married. To all the couples who struggle to find the courage to marry—even after living together—our path must seem like madness. But it was the best thing we ever did.

One small side note: your engagement should not be a social media moment. I personally abhor pictures "discreetly" taken by a "friend," at just the "right" moment, with "that beach" or "that mountain" at exactly the right angle, where he is kneeling and she is "surprised" and romantically touched. Your engagement should be a fiercely private moment between the two of you. Your marriage in church can be as public as you like. But your engagement is for you.

I know, some women will want their engagement to be a "fairytale" moment. Some may be thrilled if you ask her on camera in a full stadium with everybody watching (and bully her into accepting so as not to spoil the moment). Hey, it's your engagement.

But most women would rather have you just ask them. So decide—and ask! You can settle all the other stuff later.

Running into Trouble

If you are having a very hard time discerning about a potential marriage, if there are problems and complications—perhaps sudden, painful misunderstandings between the two of you—it is possible that this *might* be a warning sign to reevaluate your relationship. It might be a sign that the two of you are, in the end, not compatible.

Be aware, however, that if you are planning to embark on a holy marriage, open to children, with God at the heart of your relationship, you may have complications around the time of your engagement, and just before you get married, that are diabolically inspired. As a Catholic, I believe in the existence of the devil. And if there's something the devil hates and wants to prevent with all his might, it is the founding of a good, holy marriage. He will try to stop the two of you from getting together.

That is why discernment must always be done with prayer and be open to the voice of God.

But of course, most relationships are complicated, and the simple rules that I have given you will not give all the answers. What if your significant other does not have all the core characteristics, or not fully? What if your potential spouse is not the fighter for chastity whom you would love to find? What if he is only just discovering the Catholic Faith (perhaps because you are so alluring)?

We live in an unwholesome world. All of us are sinners, and many of us are wounded and have gone astray. Forgiveness and humility are important.

At the beginning, you should aim for the top of the scale. But in the moment, with God's help and grace, all is possible. So pray. He will tell you what to do.

Doubts about Marrying Young

Some people hesitate to get engaged because they've been told: "Don't get married young." It is like a dogma in their head. Getting married young, they have heard, will compromise your future. First "have fun." Then make a career and earn a lot of money—especially if you want to be able to support a family. Don't even think about marrying in your twenties, not even if you meet your perfect potential spouse.

But review my checklist. Does it contain words of caution about marrying young? It does not. If the other points check out—if you have met Mr. or Miss Right—why wouldn't you want to spend as much time as possible married to that person? I honestly can't see any argument against sharing your days as a student, or the early days of your career, married. The sooner you get married, the more your lives will intertwine.

Yes, you should probably have some idea as to how the two of you will support your life together. But you will need to support your life alone anyway—and life together costs less. Even if you have children, they are very small for the first few years and don't cost that much—not compared with the joy they bring.

Here is a final thought for you. Many women who delay marriage and having children in favor of a career find that having children later is not as easy as they expected, particularly if they want more than one and a half. A woman's body is ready for childbearing when she is quite young—much less ready when she is thirty-eight. Many women who delay having children go through terrible things such as IVF because their older bodies just don't work as those women had been told.

Engagement

It seems that getting engaged is often the most difficult step, even more challenging than getting married. Yes, on a supernatural level, marriage is a gigantic, world-changing experience. But after you are engaged, things typically get put in motion, and that helps carry you across the line.

But you are not there yet.

"What? Now that we are engaged, we can move in together, right?"

You're joking. Haven't you been listening? Your engagement shouldn't be an endlessly long affair. It should be just long enough to give you time to arrange the marriage, ideally a Catholic marriage with instruction, as requested by the Church. Your intimacy belongs—am I repeating myself?—in the lifelong, protected, safe, holy environment of a sacramental marriage. You will have years, decades to enjoy being with each other.

Don't spoil this. Be chaste.

And a second, very important thing: you are not there yet. Engagement is a time to prepare for marriage, but it is also time for further discernment. Keep speaking and praying together. You've made a decision to get married; but you haven't actually gotten married yet. Don't be afraid to question your engagement if you learn things that seriously undermine the central expectations of your future marriage.

But don't be too scrupulous. Don't root around for problems. Don't worry too much if there are small frictions and tiny misunderstandings. Those things are natural. Ask God to show you if there is a real problem. In the meantime, remember this saying attributed to Don Bosco: "Be cheerful, do good, and let the sparrows chirp."

What Kind of Wedding?

What kind of wedding? Well, clearly a Catholic wedding.

Your wedding is a sacrament, you see, a "sacred mystery." Whether it is a small family wedding with a handful of guests, or a big, expensive event on a Caribbean island with hundreds of guests, the core of marriage is about inviting the Lord into your relationship. This is the thing that will transform your friendship, your love, your relationship into something that leads to eternity.

So make sure that you get this part right. Talk about it as a couple. Ask yourselves what you would like to have in the liturgy. Wedding cakes can be burned; the floodgates of heaven can douse your garden reception (by the way, did you know it's a sign of a happy marriage if it rains on the bride's train?). But the liturgy is for eternity.

As for the rest, I can't give you too much advice anyway. Most people have a pretty clear idea about the wedding dress and which friends to invite. (For the life of me, I can't understand the fuss that is made about wedding dresses. For us grooms, the wedding is a far simpler affair.)

For what it's worth, here are a few tips from my experience:

Make sure that you plan well. But have some friends, or family, ready to take over organizational duties in the last days. I caught myself monitoring logistics *during my own wedding*—very foolish. I almost couldn't concentrate on the sacrament itself. You must let go eventually. The important thing is not smoothly functioning arrangements, or which photographer stands where, but that you ask God to enter your lives.

While we are at it, don't ruin yourself financially over a wedding. Financial stress can be a great strain on a young couple. Don't unnecessarily add to the burden.

The priest who celebrates your wedding Mass should be one who knows you both well—ideally, the priest who prepared you for marriage. Ask that the sermon be not merely about you two; encourage the priest to give a sermon that might encourage other marriages or might help couples who are having difficulties to find their way back to each other. Offer God that sermon.

Make sure that your wedding is encouraging, in general, and shows the beauty of your faith to other people. Fill it with beautiful liturgy, prayers, and music. Give the guests a chance to read along with the readings and the prayers. Perhaps their hearts will be touched. And here's a little secret: ask God, as a gift, that during your wedding, at least one new couple will find their way toward each other and marriage. Why? Because it was my experience: I was placed beside my future wife at a wedding because the bride thought, "Who knows? Those two might be a good married couple."

I know. Crazy, right? But it happened.

Consider having your wedding bands engraved, and think carefully about what to write. Bl. Emperor Karl chose the Latin prayer to Mary "*Sub tuum praesidium confugimus, Sancta Dei Genetrix*"; that is, "We fly to thy protection, O holy Mother of God." My wife and I have engraved on our rings "Jesus, Maria, Joseph." We invited the Holy Family into our lives. The engraving reminds us always of God's presence, and His Mother and her spouse.

There were hundreds of Habsburg weddings. But I want to share with you one in particular: that of Bl. Emperor Karl and Zita, in the chapel of Schwarzau Castle in Austria on October 21, 1911. This day, the day of their wedding, is the feast day that Pope John Paul II assigned to Bl. Karl when he beatified him, rather than April 1, the date of Bl. Karl's death, which is usually the date that would be chosen. The saintly pope from Poland hoped eventually to canonize this couple together, so he chose their wedding date as the day they would both be remembered. Here's another wedding wish for you: that you lead a holy married life so that your wedding date may one day be a feast day too.

You can watch online a beautiful nine-minute video clip about Karl and Zita's wedding day (just search for it). While you can't see the wedding itself, you can marvel at all the beauty that was part of it: the corteges, the arrival of the guests, and the joyful wedding reception. The couple were very young—and beaming. Zita is a pure and delightful bride in a magnificent wedding dress, and the old Emperor Franz Joseph looks happy, as he rarely did in the last years of his reign. This day was a bright ray of light. Just three years later, World War I would destroy this entire world. Bl. Karl and Zita's great friend Franz Ferdinand, who was heir to the throne, can also be seen in the background of the reception. He is in a very good mood too. No one knows that he will be assassinated in Sarajevo.

We have only one photograph of the wedding itself, in the rather small chapel of the castle. In fact, of all the hundreds of guests, only seventy, including the emperor, could be present at the wedding itself. You, too, don't need a huge church to be married in.

In the traditional rite, the marriage ceremony is before the beginning of the Holy Mass, so as not to interrupt the liturgy. This means that Karl and Zita were already married when Mass began. Papal delegate Cardinal Gaetano Bisleti read a message from Pope Pius X that is suitable for all marriages, so I quote it here: "May God protect the bride and groom, who are endowed with all virtues, in their future. May the families of the bride and groom be a constant refuge in bitter hours." No one knew how bitter, or how soon, the hours would come for Karl and Zita—and for the whole world.

The wedding lunch was a very traditional Austrian selection of dishes: lettuce with cream, St. Hubertus–style wild hare puree, Renaissance lamb roast, Parisian-style langoustine, roast turkey, seasonal salad, asparagus with butter, pineapple and strawberry ice cream, cheese, fruit, dessert.

I don't remember what was served at my wedding. But I do remember the speeches. I think that speeches are very important, though my children always dread the moment I get up to speak.

They are afraid I will get emotional. But some moments, including weddings, warrant emotion. I remember very well the beautiful things my father-in-law said about his daughter. She had already been my wife for two whole hours.

That was mind-blowing, to be honest.

So be prepared. After the wedding reception is over and you leave for your honeymoon—or your new home or your new life—you may find yourself alone in a car or an apartment or on the street and suddenly think in terror:

"What have I done?"

In fact, if you are not overawed by the greatness of what you have done, you are probably doing something wrong. You have just irrevocably changed your life forever.

But if the panic does grab you now, you will know how to handle it: pray together. And know that you have embarked on the greatest adventure of your life.

4

Being Married and Building a Family

So now you are married. Congratulations! Your courtship has ended, and your new life together has begun. Now you must build on the solid foundation that you formed together during your courtship and engagement.

The most important thing you can do is to keep praying together. But before I get to the praying part, I'd like to make a few suggestions, bits of advice gleaned from decades of practice.

First, you should constantly work on your love and relationship as spouses. When children arrive, everyday life can overwhelm you. So it is very good to develop a few habits now. Some couples reserve one evening per week to celebrate their life together, whether they go out or have a festive time together at home. (Some people call this a "date night.") Look into each other's eyes and be aware of yourselves as a couple. This will seem natural at the beginning; later on, it may take more work.

Here I want to share another wonderful secret of a good and holy marriage: the great secret about a lifelong marriage is that you have *so much time*. Many people never experience the joy of a long marriage, because their short relationships are doomed never to get there. But you have *lots of time* to get to know each other, lots of time to open up, to heal each other's wounds. You have time to discover who the other person really *is*. Your spouse is a mine of treasures with hidden secrets that might come out only after years, even decades, of being together. You will probably never know everything about each other—but that's a beautiful thing too. Life together will never get boring.

As your knowledge of each other grows, your trust will grow too. It is an incredible experience to be looked at by someone who truly loves and truly knows you—very different, by the way, from being with someone who is out to enjoy you (or your body) for a short time. It is wonderful to be looked at with truly loving eyes, to be seen, with love, through the eyes of another. (Many people are too tough on themselves.)

But lifelong love is best nourished by small gestures, time together, and gentle words. Try watching romantic comedies (or monster movies!) on your laptop while sitting on your bed. Or read novels of knightly chivalry and romance to each other—Emperor Maximilian and Princess Mary of Burgundy did.

But give yourself time apart too. Absence makes the heart grow fonder—and you'll have things to talk about when you reunite.

If either of you is hot-tempered, remember that you have plenty of time to learn how to handle each other. Archduke Franz Ferdinand (of Sarajevo fame) was well known for his irascible nature. He used to explode over small things and yell at people. But he was a devout follower of the humble Sacred Heart and well aware of his weakness. He gave his wife, Sophie, a lamb brooch and asked her to wear it always. He told her that when she noticed he was beginning to get angry—especially when he didn't notice it himself—to very discreetly touch that piece of jewelry with her finger in order to signal him. He would then try to get control of his anger. (I learned this story from a cousin of mine, a descendant of Franz Ferdinand, who now has this brooch.)

Another secret to marriage that I will share with you is not to let the sun set on a conflict. (Well, it's not really a secret. It's right there in the Bible: "Be angry and do not sin; do not let the sun go down on your anger, and give no opportunity to the devil" [Eph. 4:26–27].) That often takes humility. And, of course, people are different: some want to hash everything out; others prefer to bury things deep inside themselves. This is not an exact science. But the wonderful thing about being a married couple is that you sleep in the same bed every night of your life. It makes it difficult to avoid clarifying things before you go to sleep.

But the core thing, the most important thing, is prayer and faith. As Bl. Emperor Karl said to his wife the day after their marriage, when they visited Our Lady's sanctuary of Mariazell in Austria: "Now we have to help each other into Heaven."

In Charles Coulombe's biography of Empress Zita, you can read about how Bl. Karl and Zita tried to help each other by the way they lived their piety in their marriage:

> Fortunately, when they married, their devotional lives were already very similar. First and foremost was the Blessed Sacrament, the Holy Eucharist. Zita and Charles both loved the Liturgy of the Mass very much, attending daily and receiving as often as possible; they also loved Adoration of the Blessed Sacrament, which … would become a great consolation to them both. They were devoted to the Holy Cross—Zita in particular, as a member of the Order of the Starry Cross….
>
> … Both were also deeply devoted to the Sacred Heart of Jesus. This is a unique devotion, because of its many facets: personal, as we saw with Franz Ferdinand, who was making the Nine First Fridays and wearing a medal of the Sacred

> Heart when he was murdered; familial, because families were urged to enthrone an image of the Sacred Heart in their homes to show the Household's acceptance of Christ's rule over that family; and political.... The Imperial couple were also very devoted to Our Lady—both ... at Mariazell and other shrines, but also in the daily Rosary, either as individuals or as a family.

This was the way of life that made Charles a blessed and began Zita's cause for canonization. It also led to nine children (in eleven years), a deeply happy marriage, and a great unity in thought and outlook on the world.

Perhaps you think this is too much! Daily Mass? All those novenas and devotions? (All those children!) Speaking about the Faith all the time? Isn't that more of a monastic lifestyle? (Well, not the children part.) Shouldn't we embrace the world instead of retreating into a monastery?

But think of all the life they lived! Don't you want to be alive and live your life to the fullest? Yes, we should absolutely embrace life and the world. But we should remember that we don't stop being fragile, volatile, miserable sinners just because we've gotten married. In my experience—and I hear the same thing from many, many, many members of my family—all these religious devotions are a valuable corset (now there's an antique word) that keeps our lives in shape, the crutch that helps us walk.

But "hobbling along" is not the goal. By praying together, practicing devotions, and receiving the sacraments frequently, you invite God into your marriage. He is very discreet; He will not impose on you or your free will. But if you give Him just a little space in your schedule, He will work the magnificent wonders He has prepared for your family.

Don't forget: you are preparing for the arrival of your children. If you had a Catholic wedding, you promised to raise your children in the Faith. The best way to that do is by living this Faith yourself. Children love to imitate what their parents do, even when they resist following their orders.

So don't stop your faith journey just because you made it across the finish line to marriage. The finish line is really just the starting line for the rest of your life.

Having Children

As you know by now, our Habsburg family is large and blessed with many children. My personal family is large too (though not as large as Maria Theresia's). I strongly advocate for having children, having them *as soon as possible*, and having *many*.

Children are the greatest gift that spouses can give each other. And the greatest gift you can give your children is many siblings. A large family is a sheltering nest, a bastion of warmth, and a platoon of people who always will have your back. Having had six children was the greatest blessing my wife and I ever opened our hearts to accept. They are the heart, the core, of our happiness.

Before I delve into this topic, which is so dear to my heart, let me touch on a painful one. I know many couples among our friends who would love nothing more than to have lots of children but can't. This is such a hard and sad topic. Many marriages strain under it.

First of all, never lose hope. There are many miracles. For many families, it simply took much, much longer than expected to have a child—and you don't have to go back to Abraham to find them. I know a couple whose prayed-for child took thirteen years to arrive. Even in my family, there are couples for whom it took many years to have a child.

For example, Empress Maria Theresia's parents, Charles VI and his wife, had no children for ten years. Then two daughters arrived. In the nineteenth century, Archduke John married the love of his life, the postmaster's daughter Anna Plochl. They went on pilgrimages to Mariazell and prayed for a child for years. Finally, after ten years, they had a son. He was their only child, but today their descendants, the Meran family, number in the hundreds.

Still, there are many couples who have learned that there is no scientific hope of their having children. If this is the case for you, trust that God will give you a meaningful life in other ways. For people of faith, spreading the gospel, doing good works, and furthering the Kingdom of God make for an incredibly fulfilling life. You will have more time for those things if you are not bound by children.

But if you feel called to have children, there is a great need for foster parents and an abundance of children who are hoping to be adopted. The options vary from country to country, and from legal system to legal system. But I know many people who went through the adoption process. I also know people who adopted and then had natural children afterward.

In any case, we as Christians believe that nothing happens without God's permitting it; He has planned a special path, just for you. Have faith and trust that He loves you and desires your happiness, even if sometimes that happiness may be attained through suffering.

Lots of Children

Apart from a loving husband and wife, having many children is the surest path to a wholesome family life. Let me tell you why I think this is so.

My parents had three children, and my siblings and I were all close and got along very well, but I distinctly remember visiting relatives with four or five children and feeling a pang of envy. In fact, my mother had six siblings (in my youth, many aristocratic families were large), my father had eight, and every Christmas and Easter, when we got together with my twenty-four first cousins and our houses were teeming with children, I thought that this was the greatest thing ever. I'm sure it must account partly for my later desire to have a large family. But joy is incredibly attractive in its own right, and when we see it, it is natural to be drawn toward it. So I am grateful for the example I was given.

Of course, not all of these families always lived in complete harmony. I remember two families with five sisters, cousins to us, who I could tell often quarreled among themselves. But I also saw the wonderful way they had each other's back. What particularly impressed me was seeing such families appearing at a ball and being attracted to their strong sense of family unity.

My wife and I did not start our marriage dogmatically determined to procreate profusely. In fact, we played it by ear—or rather, by heart. After each child, we prayed and asked ourselves whether there was more space in our hearts, and in our house, for another child. There always was. In a few short years, we had six children.

The moment that captures, for me, the joy of a large family is sitting around the dinner table together. Many times over the years, surrounded by all the noise, the endless discussions, and the whirlwind of movement and energy, my wife and I have looked at each other across the table and known that we were thinking the same thing: What have we done? And how utterly wonderful!

But here's the point: watching the interactions of the siblings around the dinner table shows you how important it is for children to grow up with many brothers and sisters. You see the little six-year-old attentively watching his older sisters, adopting expressions and ideas from them. You see the youngest girl trying to speak up several times and not breaking through the endless chatter of everybody else talking at the same time. Finally, she cries and runs out of the room. You see how a sibling retrieves her, tears still drying on her cheeks. You watch as the others learn, once again, that they have to be more attentive to their younger, less forceful sisters.

I loved walking on tiptoes past the children's room at night and listening to several of them talking quietly with each other in the darkness before going to sleep, exchanging ideas, taking comfort in the presence of the others, knowing that they would always have a family and siblings who would watch out for them. All of this is still quite unconscious. But it slowly weaves the tapestry of their self-esteem and forms their outlook on life.

Watching our gang grow up—from babies to toddlers to adults (well, never *quite* adults to their parents)—and appearing, finally, at those festive balls themselves that I saw as a child has been the greatest happiness of my life.

A Gift for the Children

Some of my children are already married with children of their own; a few are still teenagers. It is only recently that I have come to appreciate what growing up in a large family gives to all involved. It is only now, when my children are beginning to disperse over countries and continents—when they meet daily no longer at the dinner table but on our little social media group—that I see the great size of this web of love, faith, companionship, and fun that God has woven in our family. If any of them ever stumble, they will be caught by God and their Faith, and also by their siblings.

We live in a time where there are so few large families that many people don't even know one and have never seen the joy that they bring. But perhaps you can see now why having a large family is the greatest gift you can give to your children.

And never worry that you won't love all your children equally. You won't. You will love them each a little differently. I know several families with nine or ten children, which is beyond even my experience. But children come one by one (or perhaps as twins, if you're lucky). So you will have plenty of time to learn the contours of your heart.

A Gift for the Parents

You will sometimes hear it said that children can compete with your love for your spouse, who is "totally exhausted" by the children. You hear that, after having children, spouses can't "enjoy each other" anymore.

While there are certainly exhausting moments and even longer exhausting times, the richness of your life with children will bring you and your spouse closer together as a couple. By having children, you and your spouse will grow into the people God always wanted you to be. I like to say that before I had children and a family life, I was like a piano player who played with just the index fingers of his two hands, and in only one octave. Through family life, I discovered that there are many octaves, that I could use ten fingers, and that there are many surprises—like pedals!—to the thing. Living, surviving, rejoicing, and crying over children bring a couple so incredibly close together that their love gets richer and richer. Honestly, that has been my experience.

And here's another little life secret: if you find it hard to handle your two children because they are so intense, have a third one. This is not my private opinion. Many, many families have confirmed this to me. Even more, three is just the sound barrier, the point after which raising children becomes easier and easier. Four, five, and six are not harder but are easier and easier. I don't know why this is so. My private theory is that two children still rely on their two parents to entertain them; and you can still lift two children up with two arms. But not three. Definitely not six. After three, the children begin to be a real gang of their own. They start to take care of themselves. And believe me, with three children, you will have less stress and more serenity.

And at the risk of repeating myself: unless you have seen it yourself, you don't know how deeply beautiful it is.

Work and Family

In many countries in the Western world, large families are now a curiosity. The attitude seems to be: "Some people have cars, some have bonsai trees, and your thing is to have many children. But that's your own private hobby. Good luck." That is grievously wrong.

Of course, there are many reasons why people don't have lots of children. For some, it is because they have never seen an example. Others think "it is simply not done" in their society. For some people, it conjures up an image of the past, when women were not free and couldn't freely work. But a main reason (for example, in Italy, where I have lived the last few years) seems to be that having lots of children is a great financial burden. Many people ask themselves: Can we afford this, or can we afford this only if both of us are working?

Given everything else that governments do these days, it seems as if they could do more, a lot more, to support families. Large families could be given subsidies, tax advantages, aid for bigger apartments or building houses. The Hungarian government has been doing this for years. Why should the state do this? To begin with, it is in the state's interest. Not only do large families raise the voters of tomorrow and the people who will pay your pensions. But as we've seen, a large family is also where people learn, by default, all of the virtues of a just, compassionate, merciful society; large families raise citizens who are ready to engage in society, take responsibility, and look after others.

But while states should certainly be prodded to support families, I also invite you to analyze closely your own thinking. Ask yourself whether having a wholesome family is your highest priority. Is an openness to having many children really part of your vision? Or is it more important to earn enough money to afford a certain status, to live in the "right places," to have "a cool lifestyle"?

Having a large family almost always involves sacrifice, but it is a sacrifice that is rewarded tenfold. You may have to move somewhere where living is more affordable. That super-cool job in that super-cool place with super-cool travel may require too much from you. You may have to drive a beaten-down, rusty old family van. That expensive vacation may have to wait.

You may even lose a few friends along the way.

But all of that is nothing—I repeat, nothing—compared with the riches, the joys, and the beauty of a large family.

Or consider this. Imagine you had five children. Now imagine you wanted a nice vacation, a bigger house, and new car. Which of your children do you imagine you would get rid of in order to have those things?

A Catholic Voice

Nobody could sum up better many of the thoughts and arguments for having many children than Pope Pius XII, who gave a wonderful talk to numerous families in 1958. Among the beautiful things he said is this central passage:

> But you do not represent just any families at all; you are and represent large families, those most blessed by God and specially loved and prized by the Church as its most precious treasures. For these families offer particularly clear testimony to three things that serve to assure the world of the truth of the Church's doctrine and the soundness of its practice, and that redound, through good example, to the great benefit of all other families and of civil society itself.
>
> Wherever you find large families in great numbers, they point to: the physical and moral health of a Christian people; a living faith in God and trust in His Providence; the fruitful and joyful holiness of Catholic marriage.[2]

Later

Just as with engagements and marriage, I often hear—even in Catholic circles—that one shouldn't rush it with children but should have them "later." It's the same story: young lovebirds should have "some time with each other" and "enjoy each other" (as if one would not enjoy each other once children arrived). Settle down, find a good home, advance your career.

But you see where this leads. If marriage is about being together and about having an intimate relationship open to life, it should be according to God's plan, not according to yours. God's plan for

[2] Pope Pius XII, "The Large Family," in *The Pope Speaks* (Spring 1958), posted on Catholic Culture, https://www.catholicculture.org/culture/library/view.cfm?recnum=5370.

you is to be fruitful and multiply, to be a family open to life—right from the beginning.

Not being open to children right away is like stretching out singlehood; it is almost like not getting married, like pretending nothing has changed. I understand these instincts. It can be a little frightening to realize that you are bound to another and that, from a certain perspective, you are less free. Why plunge even deeper into unknown territory?

But you have embarked on a great adventure, and the ultimate adventure involves babies.

I am not saying that it will be easy to have many children. It will involve a lot of planning, calculations, sacrifices, and decisions to have "less." We are used to our comforts and our freedoms. But in the end, it comes down to priorities: Do you want to have a wholesome family in an unwholesome world? Do you believe that God has called you to that vocation? If the answer to both questions is yes, then trust in it.

There's a German saying: *Schenkt der Herr ein Häschen, schenkt er auch ein Gräschen*—"If God gives a rabbit, He will also give the grass to feed it." This is an invitation not to be imprudent but to have confidence. I had my children long before being a diplomat, when I was an animation producer and a scriptwriter and worked for the Church. Those are not the sorts of jobs that make you rich.

Career Moms

Marrying and having children will lead to great changes in your life, wonderful changes. In fact, if your life isn't different since you got married, then perhaps you are doing something wrong. But you will have to think hard about the question of work and careers, especially with respect to having children.

Some people will disagree with me. But I believe that when children arrive, mothers should be at home, and not in the workplace. Everyone understands this instinctively. It is why most states, and most companies, provide maternity leave right after birth. But motherhood isn't just for a few months, right after birth. The same instinct that recognizes the need for motherhood after birth should be trusted—if possible—to structure your life as your babies grow into children and your children grow into young adults.

I know we live in a time when many people consider this idea old-fashioned or against the freedom of women or consider it an unrealizable goal,. But how can it be an unrealizable goal in a society that is enormously richer than societies in the past? And how can it be against the freedom of women, when many women say it is what they really want?

These days, it seems the only place where you can prove your worth is in the workplace. But that is a lie promoted by our corporate, consumerist society. You probably know this already, if you have read this much of my book without having thrown it angrily out the window. You probably know that a truly fulfilling life requires more than success in the corporate world and a "trophy child" at thirty-nine in order to have the "child experience." Even so, today's young women face enormous pressure to work. Most hardly dare to dream the dream of being at home and raising children. What will all my colleagues at work think? Or all my friends? That being a mother is the ultimate *failure*?

Perhaps it will help to recall that, for most of history, the greatest dream for most women was exactly this now often unthinkable thing. It is the unspoken dream of children too. Let me say this very clearly: our family is what it is, and our children are the balanced, happy, well-formed human beings they are, only because my wife decided to stop working when our first child arrived.

Family life is all-encompassing. Your children will have problems, drama, fears, and pains. They will want to speak about them immediately, whether at eleven o'clock at night or at ten o'clock in the morning or right after they get home from school. I have had working parents assure me that they had "quality time with their daughter on Wednesday afternoons." But the big drama isn't always scheduled for Wednesday afternoon. And your child wants to learn from *you* how to handle life. Do you really want to delegate this incredible responsibility to somebody else?

Mothers who stay home really get to fine-tune their understanding of the very different character of each of their children and to delight in them. But to understand how your boy or girl ticks, you have to spend time with that child, lots of time—many, many hours in the course of everyday life, often while you are doing something else. Then children learn that "Mom is here; everything is fine." They feel safe in the world and confident about growing up to be part of it.

Again, I don't wish to pressure or berate. There are often very good reasons—both economic and personal—for both parents to work. But the cultural consensus that women *should* work is so prevalent that I want to remind you that there is another way. I also invite you to question your own motivations about working. Are you doing so because you think you should or because it is really necessary? Make sure you are putting your children's happiness, and your own, above social expectations.

Consider that the formative years, in which a child shapes his ideas of the world and of love, are the first three years; and then ask yourself whether you really want to miss those magical moments and hand them off to somebody else.

If you must work, think about finding a job that you can do from home. Modern society poses many problems, particularly for women and families, but the ability to work remotely is a tremendous opportunity for women.

Perhaps it will help to give another example from Habsburg history. Is there any woman who combined work and family life more successfully than Empress Maria Theresia? She had sixteen children in twenty years and famously said: "I would have personally been on the field in the battles with Frederick of Prussia, if I hadn't been pregnant all the time." Nevertheless, she cheerfully ran and reformed a global empire—working from home.

Children with Special Needs

People often share with me this fear: What if one of our children happens to be handicapped? As many families will tell you, this will indeed add a special set of challenges to your family life. But if life, in the end, is about love, a family should be ready to embrace such a child with special love. The mark of the early Christians in antiquity was that they refused to abort their children and always cherished the poor, the sick, and the handicapped as special gifts of God. It is often the case that it is precisely a child with special needs who will bring the family closest together.

I have journalist friends in the United States who couldn't have children and wanted to adopt a child. Being Catholics, they adopted a child with special needs. A year later, the adoption agency reached out to them about another handicapped child whose birth parents specifically requested that their baby go to a Catholic family. The couple were unsure whether they had the stamina to adopt another handicapped child. They asked their spiritual director what they should do. "I don't know what you should do," he said, "but I know what you *will* do." They adopted the child—and soon after that, they had a child of their own, totally unexpectedly.

I won't say it is easy. Life with two handicapped children is challenging indeed. But these parents never wonder what the purpose of their life is. They do not suffer from modern existential angst. They are models of Christian charity, and every moment of their lives is a form of worship given to God. Their example is one of the strongest testimonies I know as to how to live such difficult questions.

Pregnancy

From the moment you receive the joyous news that you are expecting a baby, everything is transformed. Life has become something new.

The first thing you should do is talk to God about it. Give Him this new life, this little soul who has just begun his or her voyage toward eternity.

Begin to pray daily, and for the rest of your life, for your children—in their joys and woes, for their futures. God will ask you about them, so pray for them every day, even before they are born.

Bl. Emperor Karl did this so well that, even as he lay dying, he prayed for all of his children. When he slipped in and out of consciousness, he asked his wife to help him make sure he had not forgotten anyone, including the unborn child Zita was carrying ("and the small one"). Perhaps his good example will give you encouragement to do the same, every day.

I have spoken about praying together as a couple. But that is hard to do if you don't also have your own personal prayer life. Find a way to fit prayer into your day and use a form of prayer that is manageable for you in the long term. For some people, the best moments are early in the morning: I start my day praying Lauds (and drinking my coffee) before my family wakes up. Some people pray during the day, perhaps a furtive Rosary on the train on the way to work. Others wait until evening and end their day speaking to God. Some do it all. But it is very important that you figure out a form of daily prayer to keep God at the center of your life.

Wives: best to start your prayer routine now, before the arrival of the cherubic little martinet who will totally take control of your life.

Husbands: pray for strength to be chivalrous and tender when the storm comes.

Birth

The birth of your child is as profound a moment as you will ever experience. You are undoubtedly making all the appropriate worldly preparations. But do not neglect the spiritual preparations. Do not forget to give thanks to God. Birth is an intense moment, a moment almost between death and life. I have personally experienced the births of all of our six children, the last two at home. It was overwhelming to see my wife's strength and courage.

The Habsburgs have always known that birth must be given over to God and His Mother. They implored their family—and their people—to pray for those giving birth and for the safe delivery of their babies. In fact, Empress Maria Theresia ordered adoration of the Blessed Sacrament in all the churches of Vienna before every one of her births. When the future emperor Leopold II was about to be born, the Blessed Sacrament was exposed in the chapel of the Hofburg for prayer.

Before our two last children were born at home, we converted a small room into a little chapel. While things were unfolding, my other children and I were able to pop over to the chapel to pray. So even if you can't command half the country to pray for you, you can certainly pray yourself.

A small corner of your house can easily be converted into a holy space. In fact, I strongly encourage everyone to have in their house or apartment a prayer corner, a dedicated place of worship, or at least a holy image in every room—yes, even in the kitchen. In the German-speaking world, this prayer area used to be called the *Herrgottswinkel* (corner for the Lord). A prayer corner gives you the opportunity to connect with God wherever you are in your day. Flowers and a candle help beautify the space and create a prayerful atmosphere.

During the hospital birth of one of our children, the delivery room nurse remarked that it was the first time she had met a family who not only prayed in the hospital before and during the birth but also phoned family members to tell them to pray. You see, it is possible even today to follow the Habsburg faith during a birth.

And here's a thought: Many people ask for prayer over social media. I have prayed for many births (and for good deaths) because I was asked to do so. I consider it a great honor to be asked to do so.

Baptism

After birth, Baptism is usually the next big event in the life of an infant. In the Habsburg family, babies are usually baptized very soon after their birth. For instance, Leopold II was baptized the day he was born, as was his brother Archduke Charles, on September 5, 1771. The child was born around noon and was baptized in the evening.

This surprises many of us today. Isn't Baptism supposed to be the occasion for a nice big family feast that is prepared and planned for weeks? Don't we have to give time for the mother to recover from birth and for distant relatives to make travel arrangements?

For many people, Baptism has indeed become a social event rather than an expression of faith. But our Faith tells us that the single most important thing that parents can give their children is Baptism; it will enable their children to get into Heaven one day, and nothing is more important than that.

Of course, in prior eras, children were more likely to die in the very first days of their lives; nobody wanted to risk endangering the eternal salvation for the sake of a family party. But though the risk of dying is not as great today as it was two hundred years ago (thank God), the monumental importance of Baptism remains the same. That should not be forgotten, even though we are, medically speaking, so much more fortunate than our forebears. Baptism puts your baby on "Team Jesus" and on the road to eternal life. Why put that off for weeks and months?

Think, too, of all those mothers today who were ready to carry a baby to term, even though they knew the baby would not be able to survive more than a few minutes after birth—just because they wanted to be able to give that child the gift of Baptism.

In addition to binding your child to the Church, Baptism is also the formal naming of your child in Heaven. Naming a child is a big responsibility. Having had six children, I can attest that it is a really good idea to give your children names of good, impressive Christian saints (and perhaps not the name of your favorite character from *The Lord of the Rings* or *Dune*). Nearly all of our children developed relationships of friendship and devotion to their patron saints. It is an extremely rewarding experience to visit the resting place, or sanctuary, of your children's name saints: I remember when I took my son Paul for the first time to the basilica of St. Paul Outside the Walls, where St. Paul himself is buried. My son was amazed.

The First Months

You probably know that the first days, weeks, and months with a new human being are very intense. I still remember the first evening after the birth of our first daughter. I was allowed to spend the night in the hospital room with my wife while our daughter rested in her little bassinet in the corner. I peered in and saw her looking at me and thought: "You think I know what to do? I have *not the slightest clue*! I have never done this before! Your fragile little life is in the hands of two totally clueless amateurs!" She didn't seem fazed. She seemed as if she knew that everything was going to be fine. Mommy and Daddy were really there. Their voices were much easier to hear now.

You probably underestimate how fast you will learn. But do try to rest when you can. Sleep deprivation takes a big toll, particularly over longer periods of time. You may begin to appreciate why communist regimes tortured prisoners, such as Cardinal Mindszenty, with sleep deprivation and why they were often able to break them in that way. In your life so far, you were probably able to sleep nearly every night, unless you were partying or traveling or ill. Not anymore.

Mothers bear the brunt of it. The helpless, demanding, unreasonable new family member doesn't care how tired you are. You are the grown-up, and you must provide. There is no magical incantation to get a baby to sleep (though Mommy's voice sometimes helps). You will just have to survive it.

And you will.

You will also get an entirely new appreciation for what your parents did for you. You may never have thought about it before. Your first memories of your parents usually begin many years after birth. You do not remember the night vigils, the screaming, the insecurity, the tensions, the slightly dreamlike hue that hung over everything. The most you might recall are the first months with new siblings, when perhaps you noticed that your mother and father seemed usually tired. But you probably didn't even notice that. In any case, there is nothing quite like being there yourself now and knowing what was done for you.

If you find it challenging, remember that you are not the first human family to have experienced this. And you will not be the last. You are now part of an endless chain of parents and children. You are linked to the most fundamental human experience. Our forebears raised babies under dire and difficult circumstances. Compared with them, we live in paradise. But, like them, you don't need any special training. It's part of your basic toolkit, part of who you are.

It is, of course, a new kind of adventure. So summon up your pioneering spirit. Traversing the sea was hard for the pioneers. But they did it for a reason: for the promised land beyond it.

Remember, too, that these days will pass. (Part of you will miss them when they do; life is so vivid.) So tough it out. As a Spanish girl said to some of us at a ball when we wanted to go home to sleep: "*Ustedes pueden dormir la próxima semana*" (You can sleep next week).

But before the days do pass, take the time to look at your baby—the incredible new member of your family who has been with you for months and you can now see. Notice the little face, the tiny fingers, the wispy tufts of hair. Marvel at how your baby looks at you and learns about the world by looking at you. Begin to appreciate the beauty of your child. And begin to notice the first glimpses of his or her character. Try to make your baby smile!

But also don't expect to be immediately in love with this tiny, wrinkly, alien turtle who slowly blinks at you and makes funny faces, trying to figure out who you are. Don't be impatient for explosive happiness and feelings. Some lucky people may have this immediately; for most, it comes more slowly. Let it. It will.

When you have your second child, you will be astonished at how incredibly different human beings are, from their very first days. Man and woman, baby and baby. We have five daughters and one son, and our son is *very* different from his sisters.

Friends

In such an important, absorbing new phase of life, in addition to prayer it is very helpful to have friends—mostly for advice. So much that is happening is new. Why is your baby still crying? What if your milk doesn't come? Do I call the doctor if the baby has diarrhea? Do I have to worry if my baby has fever (spoiler: almost never). What can I do when the baby's teeth start coming in (answer: not much—sorry).

Ideally, your most helpful friends will be your own parents. If you're lucky enough to live nearby, moms and dads can even watch your child for a while at night so you can sleep for a few blessed hours.

Your siblings, too (if your parents gave you some), can help—especially if they have children of their own.

But what you often need most is just someone to talk to, sometimes urgently. Many things will seem quite daunting when you have had very little sleep. A short conversation with someone you trust will usually give you comfort and help you to relax.

Of course, the Internet can be a source of information as well. There are resources for everything available at your fingertips—more than ever were available in any royal palace. And much advice is presented by other wholesome families—though be mindful that you live in a broken world: there is plenty of crazy stuff out there too.

But as for friends, you should probably be prepared to lose a few. Some of your friends will have neither the patience nor the time to accept the new reality in your life. They will want everything in their lives to remain the same; they won't be able to join you on this new adventure. That's okay. It is understandable too. Those who have never experienced parenthood can find it very difficult to appreciate why you suddenly want to talk only about babies.

Not all friendships are destined to last forever—though some can survive a pause, even a very long one.

But don't worry: you'll make new friends. It is a great joy to discover new people and make new friends whom you can talk to about your new experiences with your new arrival.

Prayer and Love

It is very important to continue focusing on the two pillars of your marriage that we discussed above: maintaining your prayer life, both as individuals and as a couple, and nourishing your loving relationship as a couple.

The great thing about mechanical prayers such as the Rosary is that they can be said even while you carry a sleepless child around. (God was thoughtful enough to give us ten fingers that we can use in place of rosary beads.) When you are exhausted and want to sob because you don't know how to handle it anymore, you, as a Christian, can offer it up for the baby or for your spouse or for the souls in Purgatory (or perhaps for the babies who were never born).

I remember one Maundy Thursday night when I was carrying a baby who couldn't sleep. I imagined being on the Mount of Olives and seeing Jesus in agony and in prayer. Then I imagined Jesus praying in the corner of the room, and as I rocked the baby, I imagined I was trying to console Jesus in His suffering—"Whatever you did for one of the least of these brothers and sisters of mine, you did for me" (see Matt. 25:40)—and a tough moment was transformed into a spiritual experience.

Try also to pray with your spouse and, most of all, to thank God for the gift of the incredible miracle in your life. It was only when we had our first baby that, for the first time, I really appreciated these magnificent words of Jesus: "A woman, when she is in labour, hath sorrow, because her hour is come; but when she hath brought forth the child, she remembereth no more the anguish, for joy that a man is born into the world" (John 16:21, Douay-Rheims). Even Jesus remarked on the joy of the arrival of a new human being.

Also, resume going to Holy Mass as soon as possible after a baby is born. For a time, it may be possible only to read the readings and the prayers of the Mass alone at home, or perhaps you and your spouse can take turns going to Mass. But as soon as you can, go to Holy Mass again, together, and take your child along with you. It is good for your family. It is good to be together.

As for nurturing your relationship with each other, it can be a challenge. Time is often in short supply. Both your bodies are sleep-deprived, and childbirth and nursing put an added strain on mothers. Hormones take mothers on a roller coaster of changing emotions, including maternal baby blues in the first few weeks after the birth.

Don't worry. The blues will not last forever. But it can take a while for things to settle down. In the meantime, you are not exactly in the most romantic of moods. So do what you can to bring romantic moments back into your life. Even in the first weeks and months, when you are most harried, you need to remind each other that you are a couple. Set some time apart for yourselves when you can. Simple things work. Order something in to eat; watch a movie while sitting on your bed (with the crib in the corner). Flowers and gifts are helpful too. Be patient, but do work on it. It's good training for the rest of your life anyway, especially if you are fortunate enough to have several more children.

Educating Children

The first point I want to make about educating children may seem almost silly. But it is very important. This is your chance to imprint all the things that you really love on your children! Have you ever really thought about the incredible power you have been given? For example, if you play your favorite cheesy country songs from the eighties for your infants, who are lying helpless on their backs with no prior tastes of their own, they will love those songs all their lives! You can force your children to love something as cringeworthy as Barry Manilow. Or Dolly Parton! Ha! I can personally attest that it has worked several times—mostly with my elder daughters and also with my son. Some of them still have Beatles songs and Pink Floyd's "Shine On, You Crazy Diamond" in their playlists, just because I played those songs for them when they were so young. (The best part is, they still believe this is their own taste in music.)

But of course, what goes for psychedelic music goes just as well for the (arguably) more important principles of education. My father was fond of saying, "The education of a child is completed at three years." While this may seem a bit provocative, there is something to it. Children's outlook on the world, their idea of God, their sense of love, their security, their virtues, their belief about whether they have worth—all of these are shaped in those very first years of life.

You really must approach your children's education conscientiously. Come up with a plan with your spouse. Talk about what is important to you and your spouse and then try, as well as you can, to implement your goals once your child is ready to learn.

Of course, it is well said that no plan survives the first enemy contact. You shouldn't have too many precise ideas, especially with your first child. In fact, you will probably have a tendency to "experiment" a bit too much. Even so, it is good to consider early what your priorities are, what is important to you.

As I mentioned, you will find, if you have more than one child, that it is quite astonishing how incredibly different children are, even in the same family. While the general contours may remain the same, it is rare that one-size-fits-all education works. That's why you probably shouldn't trust the current "hot education book" too much (including the one you are holding now). Rather, you should try to tailor education to encourage each child's strength. And in every case, education needs to be age-appropriate.

Maria Theresia thought a lot about the very different characters of her children. We know, for instance, that she was always painfully aware that she had pampered her eldest son, Joseph (which is understandable after an entire generation without male heirs; he was the first boy to be born to the House of Austria in sixty years). She believed her coddling had turned him into a stubborn person and a rebel (who, against her wishes, secretly read Voltaire).

So don't just think about how your children will learn their facts and figures. Keep their moral education at the forefront. Remember: this is *your* marriage and *your* family. With the help of God, you and your spouse, together, will figure out what is best, what is right, and what to do.

Living Your Faith

My father has another saying, and I saw the wisdom behind it when my wife and I had our own children: as far as education, "your children won't do what you tell them to do; *they will do what they see you doing yourself.*" If you tell them that they shouldn't watch TV, but they see you watching TV all the time, they will watch TV all the time. The same goes for faith.

The way you raise your kids, from the earliest ages, should be centered on your Faith. And it is most important that your children see how you are living your Faith.

For example, when my wife was young, every morning she heard her father walk quietly past her bedroom door to go to morning Mass. He never forced her to come along. She just knew that he got up early and went humbly to Mass—on weekdays too, not just weekends. For her, this was the beginning of a lifelong love for the Holy Mass. At some point, she began going to daily Mass herself.

If children see their parents naturally praying in the morning, at lunch, or in the evening; if they see their father always carrying in his pocket a rosary (and using it); if they see their mother slipping out quietly for an afternoon prayer session in a nearby church—this is what will shape their own behavior. If something tragic happens in the family, and children see that their parents instinctively turn to prayer, they will also do this later in their lives.

Older siblings are also powerful role models. To this day, while they sometimes seek out my wife and me, our children prefer to talk about certain aspects of faith with their older siblings. They also take cues from their older sister: they see her with a rosary in her pocket, and they clamor for one for themselves.

But in addition to the power of example, it is also very important that faith is conveyed by both parents in other ways that are clear and memorable. Let me give two examples of Habsburg family members who left a deep impression on their children, to encourage you to do likewise in your family.

One of the most impressive figures in Habsburg history is that champion of the Counter-Reformation, Ferdinand II. He was deeply devout all his life, and while I can't prove that the following scene determined his character, it was definitely memorable. Ferdinand's father, Archduke Charles of Styria, had married the deeply devout Maria Anna of Bavaria. Not only did she attend three Masses every day, but she gave her husband Charles fifteen children. She also taught her son Ferdinand to kneel and fold his hands when the Angelus bells rang every day at noon, even before he knew the Angelus prayer by heart. One day, Charles promised a Protestant aristocrat that he would attend his Protestant service. Shortly after making that promise, when Charles stepped into his room, he found his wife with young archduke Ferdinand and a suitcase. Charles asked, "And where exactly are you going with the boy, my dearest?" Maria Anna answered, "I will bring him to Bavaria, my home, as it looks as if here the eternal salvation of his soul may be endangered." Charles never again thought of going to a Protestant service.

I can only imagine the impression that that scene must have made on Ferdinand. It highlights the great power that mothers have to teach the Faith.

After this confrontation, both parents came to the conclusion that Graz, with its strong Protestant culture, was not a good place for the Habsburg boy to be educated. They decided, together, to send him to a Jesuit school in Ingolstadt in Bavaria, where Ferdinand became the devout fighter for Catholicism that he remained all his life. This demonstrates the importance of spouses working together to emphasize the Faith.

If the faith of your children is endangered by their education, you have to think about unconventional solutions. I believe strongly that the key figure in passing on the Faith to children is most often the father. It makes a deep impression on children when they see that their father is leading the way—with respect to many things, but particularly the Faith.

But fathers do not have to be perfect Catholic dads to have a good influence on the faith of their children. Franz Stephan of Lorraine, the husband of the devout Maria Theresia—and the only Freemason in the Habsburg family—was a somewhat worldly bon vivant. In his letters, he rarely speaks about faith or the Church and is quite critical of the Jesuits and their spirituality. But he set a very clear example to his children with respect to the sacrament of Confession. The Duke of Lorraine understood clearly that there was a fight going on in man. He wrote to one of his children that "in every soul, there is a deadly fight happening between the devil and the guardian angels." So he encouraged his children to go to Communion often but only in combination with going to Confession every week. And he was a worthy model in going to weekly Confession himself.

His children must have been impressed by this example. After his death, Maria Theresia wrote and told one of the children to go to Confession often, ideally weekly, "as you know your father always did and exhorted you to do." She reminded them that, although their father had died unexpectedly, God had granted him the grace of having gone to Confession that very morning.

Be that father. Be that example children see in line for Confession. (You don't have to emulate Franz Stephan in being a Freemason.)

Of course, when thinking of Habsburg fathers who gave a good example in the Faith, one cannot help but think of Bl. Karl, for whom faith always had the first place in his soul. His children had him with them for only eleven short years. But for the rest of their lives, they remembered having long conversations with him, saying common prayers and the Rosary; they remembered their father explaining to them the central mysteries of the Faith, the Holy Mass, the meaning of Christ's suffering on Good Friday and His Resurrection on Easter. And they remembered being taken to eucharistic adoration by him and sharing its beauty with him.

A regular and faithful prayer and sacramental life, demonstrated from the beginning, will help your children to develop their own spiritual strength. Everything should be age-appropriate, of course, but not childish. Children can be very grown-up with respect to matters of faith at a surprisingly young age.

Fixed times for prayer can be particularly helpful. Children should begin the day with a short prayer, suitable for their age. One practice that united young Ferdinand II in the sixteenth century and Marie Antoinette in the eighteenth century was the ironclad rule that, immediately after leaving their beds, they knelt down and said a short morning prayer. Lunch and dinner can also be accompanied by prayer. Evening prayer should be a daily, calming, beautiful experience.

With smaller children, you can sing or say a little learned prayer. As they grow older, you can add a silent examination of conscience and additional adult prayers. We usually segued from prayer time to story time, so children looked forward to this peaceful time in the evening. And like my many-greats-grandfather Emperor Ferdinand I, I blessed my children with holy water every evening when they lay in bed.

Being Catholic means taking your children to church early on, as soon as possible, in fact. Don't believe the myths that children are "too small" or "can't appreciate" liturgy. Going to Mass is an experience that works its grace on you every time.

It's true, going to Mass when your children are babies requires flexibility. Having gone to Mass with my six children from the beginning, I am well aware that, in many parishes, the tiniest bit of noise attracts stares. But if one parish is not welcoming, you can always look for another; your family's spiritual health, and your children's spiritual education, are too important to be hampered by stares.

Your children should get used to going to Mass at least every Sunday, and if possible, at least once during the week. Ideally, your church will be more than just a community experience of gathering;

it will be a place where Holy Mass is celebrated devoutly, in a way that furthers your relationship with God.

If it seems like a challenge to find such a church, consider that there are families who decide to move to a different town or even a different state in order to be close to a parish and a community where the liturgy is shaped in a way that brings them closer to God. Many families make great sacrifices for the sake of beauty, reverence, and a rich sacramental life. A growing number of people, often young people, prefer the Traditional Latin Mass. For others, a "charismatic" parish feeds their soul. Some even seek out devout monastic communities. But there are modern Mass parishes, too, that are spiritually rich and reverently devout. Just be sure that the church you attend is helping you and your children grow closer to God. You want to enter into that great Mystery that is the Creator of Heaven and earth. If the community is also welcoming and has a great coffee hour, all the better.

Ideally, you will find a church that offers Masses during the week and regular Confession times. As soon as possible, children should make Confession a part of their religious life. This is much easier if they see their parents—particularly their father—and older siblings going to Confession. Teach them that Communion and Confession are connected and go together. Be firm about these things. Never forget that these sacraments nourish your family's spiritual life.

Faith is not just something that is shaped on Sundays. Stay aware of the seasons of your Faith. For instance, your family life should be different during Lent. Observe Advent and save Christmas for Christmas. Worship at home with prayers appropriate to the season.

Practice devotions such as novenas, which span days or even weeks. Start wearing the Brown Scapular. It is a helpful reminder, every time you get dressed, of your friendship with Our Lady.

Make the beautiful habit of pilgrimage part of your life. Find out which Marian shrines are near you, and develop the habit of driving there with your children while reciting the Rosary. (The Marian shrine near the Austrian Habsburgs was the sanctuary of Mariazell.) Even in the United States, there are a number of places that have Bl. Emperor Karl shrines, with relics. You can find these shrines listed on the homepage of the Bl. Karl Prayer League. Emperor Karl is a great friend to have if you hope to have a large devout family.

As I've told you, it was the example of both my parents that formed my faith. They did not simply take us to Mass on Sundays. They themselves went often during the week. They also encouraged us to go to Confession, and they went themselves. And, yes, they took us on pilgrimages.

In the end, it's surprisingly simple: show your children the beauty of the Rosary, pilgrimages, and devotions early, and they will stick with them for life. As it says in the book of Proverbs, "Train up a child in the way he should go, and when he is old he will not depart from it" (22:6).

To this day, I love encountering the many tiny sanctuaries of Our Lady and of the saints—often a simple image on a house or a little stone shrine—that I find whether I'm in the center of Rome or in the villages and countryside of Central Europe. So teach your children to make prayer walks and bring Our Lady flowers. This is a very simple way of nurturing the love of God even in small children. I know that such public places of devotion are less common in the United States. Why not make one, by hanging a painting or an icon on the outside of your house or placing a statue in your yard and putting flowers there regularly? Just an idea. Your children will thank you. Your neighbors might too. At least they'll be intrigued.

I often hear that one shouldn't overwhelm children with "too much faith"—that it could be oppressive and lead children to reject the Faith later on. That's possible, I suppose. But based on my very humble experience, I'd say the risk is small—especially if your own faith is genuine. If children sense hypocrisy, they will rebel. If they see love, they will love too.

In my stormy years, between ages thirteen and eighteen, my parents' strong renewal of their faith irritated me immensely. But even so, faith was growing inside me. Adolescence passed, as it tends to do. When I became an adult, my parents' faith helped me find my own. And parenting with my wife has taught us both that full immersion in the full richness of the Catholic Faith is the best way to guarantee that your children will have a lifelong friendship with Jesus.

I believe that the Church today will be renewed by praying families. We are suffering today from crises of faith, of vocations, of leadership. The surest way to heal and repair our Church—perhaps the only way—is through family prayer. Our pastors are tired, overworked, and overwhelmed. Sometimes they seem hopeless. It will be faithful families who will bring real, lived, devout faith back to parishes, dioceses, and Mother Church. The small, routine, everyday manifestations of faith—attending the Holy Sacrifice of the Mass, going regularly to Confession, praying the Rosary—will reignite the fire of faith in a generation of strong, hopeful, believing Catholics who will one day grow up to be the light of the world.

Family Values

The easiest, best, most effective way to have a wholesome family is to have a large family. Without too much preaching by parents, children will learn all they need to know. Let me explain.

In our family, we had a rule that the youngest child would always get served first at mealtimes. The bigger children were often a lot hungrier and usually frantic to eat first. But they had to wait until the weakest was served. They learned the values of patience, obedience, and generosity of spirit, without even knowing it.

Automatically, children in large families learn to share (even if they hate to share), and they come to see that they can't have everything they want. It's expensive to have a large family. Invariably children learn to wear hand-me-down clothes and to share toys. They will dream of having their own stuff, their own shiny new things. But in the meantime, they will learn a sense of wonder and restraint and hopefulness—and gratitude, when they finally do get things of their own—which do incredibly good things for their characters.

In a large family, the parents simply cannot do everything for their children. The next generation must take over household tasks, in age-appropriate ways, even when they are very young. The sooner you include your younger children in household chores, the better your life will be, and the better their lives will be.

In fact, if you don't do this, you will become a slave to your children and deprive them of a most important life lesson: life is not a luxury hotel where everybody caters to your wishes. Rather, a family is a miniature society in which everyone has to contribute.

Interestingly, despite their imperial grandeur, a Spartan-inspired lifestyle was always a high educational ideal of the Habsburg family. Children were often given simple food, such as sour beer and black bread, so they would learn not to make a fuss about food. Even when the food was better, portions were small to teach the princes to be satisfied with a little. Leopold II's wife taught her children, and the women in the duchy of Tuscany, to do at least some manual work. She valued productivity, and she maintained that conversations went better while one mended a basket or did some stitching.

Habsburg sons and daughters were also raised to respect their parents. They had to stand until their father allowed them to sit down. They also had to kiss the hand of the emperor when they saw him—and their father's hand too. (Ah, those were the days!)

Ferdinand I worked hard to raise his sons well. In a letter written to his sons in 1547, for instance, he quoted a psalm: "How good and pleasant it is when brothers dwell in unity" (Ps. 133:1). Don't be in conflict with each other, he taught them, because the court will use this against you. If one of your brothers offends you, accept small slights with humility. "I myself do this often, my sons." God, he reminds them, will reward such a behavior in eternity.

Ferdinand was pained by the behavior of his eldest son, Maximilian II. He saw him squandering time with too much singing and even "playing with a bear." He accused him of participating in drinking bouts, having immoral friends, and partying frivolously in Munich. When Maximilian disobeyed a direct order, Ferdinand even put his frustrations into a poem:

> *Qui asino et cervo se crede*
> *al saltar del fosco si vede.*
>
> He who is an ass but thinks himself a stag
> Should refrain from trying to jump a ditch.

He also admonished his son with the example of King Solomon's son, Rehoboam, who followed the counsel of young men rather than wise men and whose antics ultimately led to division in the kingdom of Israel.

Despite his father's efforts, Maximilian lost his way. He became a womanizer and a very "Protestant" Catholic. Still, his father's suffering and praying ultimately bore fruit. When Maximilian got married, he renounced his immoral life and remained faithful to his wife all his life. They had fifteen children together.

Leopold II (who lived in Mozart's time) was scrupulous about his children's honesty. He did not tolerate lying. He said that he wanted to give his children "a solid religious faith, based on conviction and real piety of the heart. We try to shape, in all of our children, an upright, straight, honest, and merciful heart."

The children also had to learn early on to grow up. For example, Ferdinand I encouraged his young son Maximilian II to give a public speech in Latin.

Speaking of your relationship with your children, perhaps I should highlight the importance of spending time with them—all of them together and each of them individually. This is easy and automatic in the beginning: children are cute and demand attention (loudly!) if they don't get it. But as time races by, and life gets cluttered with responsibilities, other things can seem more important.

But children need parents around, their own parents, both their fathers and their mothers. Boys and girls are incredibly different, but they both need both parents. Having had five daughters myself, I could go on for hours about the importance of fathers to their daughters. Fathers shape their self-esteem and their relationships with God, with other men, with themselves. Lack of love from, and closeness to, their father can lead daughters to try to replace that missing love with early relationships with boys—which leads to all the turmoil involved with that choice.

At the same time, boys need a man to emulate and to love, if they are to grow up to be men themselves. That's why I tried to have a very close relationship with my son, who didn't have it easy, as the only son in the family and with five sisters (*beato fra le donne*, "blessed among women," as the Italians liked to joke). A great help was a saying of my grandfather: "Raise your son so he is afraid neither of a Rosary nor of a glass of good wine."

To know your children, you have to spend time with them. Some of them might demand sufficient attention on their own, even after they are babies. But others withdraw into their own little shells, close their doors, and never ask to be noticed. Those are the ones you have to look after with particular care, the ones you have to go to yourself.

Some children will be more like you, some more like your spouse. It is important that you and your spouse converse about your children regularly so you will both understand what is in their hearts. You may be exhausted after work and have little desire to admire the piece of art your child has carefully created in his or her room. But when your spouse tells you how proud of it that child is, you must go and admire it. It shows your child that you love him or her.

Culture

It is a great joy to share your passions with your children and to transmit your family culture. Ideally, it should be done in a way that lets your children discover for themselves the things you love. For example, a visit to a museum is much more effective, and fun, than a parent's long lecture about an abstract topic.

But one of the best things you can share is the books that you love. As you read your favorite stories to them, your children's minds will develop before your very eyes; they will acquire a love for language and a feeling for ideas.

If one spouse or the other enjoys reading more, it is perfectly fine to have a designated family reader. When I was young, my mother read me stories; in my family, I have been reading to our children for the last twenty-eight years.

One benefit of a daily reading ritual is that you will very likely pass on to your children a lifelong love for books. You can't force this. Some children simply won't take to it. But in my experience, reading every evening starts them on a voyage—and develops their facility for language as well. If you have good books lying around, you'll be amazed at how quickly your children will pick them up and start reading themselves, particularly if they have older siblings to encourage them.

Still, take care that the books they read are age-appropriate. Don't force books you love on your young children if they are frightening, depressing, or too grown-up. I made that mistake several times. I traumatized some of my children by dropping the often grim *Leatherstocking Tales* onto them when they were far too young! It is always better to err on the side of caution. Listen to your children when they say, "This is weird, Dad." And remember, in the evening, children want to hear something nice and wholesome. After all, they need to sleep afterward. Dramatic adventures and thrilling tales of derring-do are better suited for Saturday afternoon.

Start with picture books for small children, and work your way up to the classics—the beloved books you read in your childhood. Don't forget to ask your parents what were classics in their day. Classics are usually classic for a reason. But be mindful as well that times change, and some twenty-first-century children find *Alice in Wonderland*, deservedly a classic, hard to appreciate and pretty weird (it is!).

You can also find online lists of wholesome children's books. I regularly ask social media followers for reading suggestions for teenage girls who liked *Anne of Green Gables* and *Betsy-Tacy*. (In general, I would avoid most of what has been written in the last few decades, unless your goal is to indoctrinate your children with the latest fad.)

Also, make sure your children read the original, unexpurgated editions of books. Many publishers now edit older books to make them "more relevant for today's children." This Orwellian impulse is not only a clumsy insult to truth (the past is what it is, whether we like it or not), but it invariably makes a story worse. If the *Little Women* you find on the shelf is surprisingly slim, there's a good chance it has been given "the treatment."

One classic that I never quite warmed to is *The Wind in the Willows*. I tried to read it to several of my children. Their reactions were always muted. But if you do want to read this classic to your kids, be sure to have the full version. In several recent editions, an entire chapter was simply dropped. Why? I think it is because it is religious. It is titled "The Piper at the Gates of Dawn." It is actually a bit pagan, but it is also one of the most hauntingly beautiful texts ever written. (Pink Floyd titled their first album after it.) And it is simply dropped in many new editions.

Fortunately, older editions are readily available on eBay and in secondhand shops. Missing chapters aside, these older volumes are usually far more beautiful than newer ones anyway, and they are often less expensive. But even if they cost a few more bucks, beauty is something of value and is worth having. Treasure the originals, and don't let them be forgotten or destroyed (as in Ray Bradbury's haunting dystopia, *Fahrenheit 451*, which, by the way, is deservedly a classic).

Another thought: consider audio versions of classical books. You can play these on long car trips, while painting or doing chores, or simply during cozy evenings at home with the family. To this day, our children quote lines and hum melodies from audiobooks they heard when they were young. I am certain that someday they will share these same joys with their own children.

Traditions

Passing on your family's traditions and rituals is of immense importance. From the way birthdays and name days are celebrated to the particular foods that are served at great feasts, traditions include all "the ways things are done in our house." These small things will do a great deal to help shape your children's identities and give them a sense of security and belonging that they will have for the rest of their lives.

The Habsburgs (as a Catholic and Central European house) have always taken very seriously family Christmas traditions. In fact, you may be surprised to hear how many Christmas traditions were introduced into Austria through the wife of a Habsburg.

We know exactly when and how this happened: in 1815, when Archduke Charles (about whose happy marriage we have already heard) married Henriette von Nassau-Weilburg. Henriette was much younger than Charles. She was also a Protestant—but that was the reason she brought a German Protestant custom to Austria. For Christmas in 1816, the year her first daughter was born, she set up the first Austrian Christmas tree in her house, in the center of Vienna. There were twelve candles on the tree, one for each of the twelve months of the year, and decorations that she had sent for from home. The custom was observed slightly critically by Charles's more traditionally minded brother John (of Styria), but the fashion soon swept across Habsburg lands.

By the way, long before the familiar Christmas traditions took hold, the feast of St. Nicholas had been celebrated in the Habsburg household. There is a magnificent painting from about 1745, painted by one of the young archduchesses, depicting a St. Nicholas celebration by the family of Maria Theresia: the emperor sits in his morning coat, the empress sips hot chocolate, "Mimi" (Marie Christine)—the painter—brings gifts, Marie-Antoinette plays with a doll, and Maximilian and Ferdinand are holding the switch used by St. Nicolas to punish bad children.

Across the centuries, Christmas always played an important role in family life, though in different ways. Following is a description of a melancholy Christmas at Eckartsau in Austria, after Karl and Zita's family was deposed from their throne in 1918. Karl was ill, but they still saw to it that the tradition was carried out. Zita (as quoted by Charles Coulombe) remembered it as follows.

> However, we did our best to make it a cheerful occasion. We had a Christmas tree, of course, on the evening of the twenty-fourth and at the foot of it we spread our pile of little gifts. We had found at Eckartsau a trunk we had once used on our official journeys which was nearly full of minor presents and this came in most useful. To the staff I remember we gave mostly the things they wanted most—bits of chocolate and other scraps of food we had saved and wrapped up for the occasion.
>
> The emperor got up for Christmas Eve but was so weak that he had to remain seated in an armchair while the presents were being exchanged. He was quite exhausted afterwards and his temperature went up again. That same night, we heard, there were toasts drunk to the emperor that night all over the capital.

Many families have their own Christmas rituals. In fact, one of the first things my family and I try to find out about potential future sons-in-law is how exactly Christmas is celebrated in their family—and there is always the looming question of how much of "their" Christmas traditions our children will manage to get in their future marriages. (They know that all is fair in love and war and that a compromise with other Christmas traditions is unthinkable. I'm kidding, of course. Or am I?)

Another old Habsburg tradition is musical and theater performances presented by children and grandchildren to parents and grandparents. For instance, as early as 1745, the children performed a French comedy, with a ballet, German dances, and a minuet. In 1752, young Leopold and his siblings studied and performed a complicated French *comedie en trois actes*. Many of the children in the play were younger than ten. In July 1756, the Habsburg troupe performed another French comedy, played it twice per week, and presented it regularly whenever guests visited Schönbrunn Castle.

Children also learned instruments and gave little concerts. For Emperor Franz Stephan's name day in 1759, they put on a show. Archduke Ferdinand performed a solo on drums; the youngest, Archduke Max, could only contribute the felicitations. Maria Antonia (later Marie Antoinette of France) sang French Vaudeville songs; other children sang Italian arias; Archduke Charles played the violin; and the future Emperor Joseph played the violoncello. They were all accompanied, on the piano, by their sisters Maria Anna and Maria Christine. You need to have a large family to organize an entire children's orchestra!

These musical traditions have been maintained for centuries. My grandfather, Archduke Joseph, remembered a performance in Schönbrunn Castle in 1908 that featured lots of archdukes and archduchesses. It was for the jubilee of Emperor Franz Joseph and had been prepared and rehearsed for a month. The rehearsals must have been something: my grandfather described improvised battles between several young Habsburgs, who regularly got into wild fights and rolled on the floor. A servant who was bringing cakes during an intermission was attacked by the children and knocked to the floor. "The dynasty with a glorious past," writes my grandfather, "was transformed into a tribe of savages."

Even so, the presentation on the evening of December 2 was magnificent. Professionals from the Vienna Opera Ballet had arranged the choreography for the little band of performers. There were recitations and music and dance. The emperor, with his white beard and his gentle eyes, was transfixed by the performance. But the end of the evening was poignant. A beautiful Habsburg archduchess told a touching fairy tale about a king that was an allegory about the aging emperor. The king in the fairy tale had many crowns, but one of them was a crown of thorns. It signified all the sufferings that Franz Joseph had endured for his people. The emperor was moved to tears.

Suddenly, a young man lifted his voice in the middle of the performers and called out: "And thus ends our joyous performance!" It was Archduke Karl, the future blessed and emperor.

Performing plays and giving concerts for parents are old traditions. But they are also great exercises in family unity and fun projects to do together. A performance doesn't have to be a ballet choreographed by professionals from the Hofburg or an entire Shakespeare play. But watching your children perform for you even one scene that they have practiced from *A Midsummer Night's Dream* is magical.

Of course, your family life is a play of its own—and birthdays are some of the best scenes. No doubt your family already has its own traditions for birthday celebrations, so I won't regale you with others here. But I would encourage you to celebrate these feasts sumptuously and always the same way. This gives children security, identity, and a tradition to carry on into their own families when they grow up. They will remember that the birthday child was always awakened in a special way; that he or she was called into the birthday room; that everyone danced around the lucky child or gave speeches. These rituals are especially important in a large family because they give every child a special moment to be the center of attention and to be celebrated at least once a year. So protocol must be respected! Children love it and feel safe and secure when things are done exactly the way they have always been done.

School and Homeschool

The world has always suffered from the effects of Original Sin—and historically, it has always been a struggle to have a wholesome family life in a decadent society. Even so, in our current times, it is increasingly becoming a challenge, especially with respect to education.

In recent years, many schools have become ideological battlegrounds where serious indoctrination according to the secular catechism takes place. Current hot ideas and fads, particularly with respect to sexual exoticism and an atheistic worldview, are compulsory parts of school life and the curriculum. In addition, the ubiquitous presence of cell phones and social media inundates kids with toxic images and ideas.

In days of yore (when I was young and went to school), there was a popular idea that children needed to experience "the world as it is today." This was thought especially true for "idealistic Catholics" who "had no idea what the real world looks like." Such experience was imperative so that children would be able to "face reality" when they grew up. Perhaps there was some truth to this thinking: an inoculation against a disease can indeed do some good.

But in our contemporary world, this notion should at least be open to doubt. Infecting your children is a dangerous business. Sometimes it is far wiser to protect them as long as possible from pathological ideologies that have the potential to cause permanent harm.

Parents usually have three choices for educating their children: (a) public school, (b) private school, and (c) where it is legal, some form of homeschooling.

If you can find a great school with a sound curriculum and reliable teachers, well done. But most schools find it hard to resist well-funded lobbies and pressure groups. Be vigilant and make sure you know exactly what your children are being taught.

In any case, education should begin at home, long before school, and should be accompanied from home all through school. Everything you want your children to learn about the world, history, culture, art, politics, and values should be actively discussed around the dinner table, on trips, on walks. This will give your children a fighting chance to survive the onslaught of indoctrination, if and when it comes.

It will be easier if your children have several siblings. The youngest will hear about the world from their more knowledgeable brothers or sisters, and the oldest will feel comforted by their younger siblings' innocence. But all will express strong opinions. Even if they are slightly shaken by encountering "the world out there," they probably won't be blown over if they feel safe at home. In one of my favorite books in the world, *Fahrenheit 451*, Captain Beatty knows exactly why they are nervous about the "dangerous" influence of family:

> You can't rid yourselves of all the odd ducks in just a few years. *The home environment can undo a lot you try to do at*

school. That's why we've lowered the kindergarten age year after year until now we're almost snatching them from the cradle. (emphasis added)

In any case, if your children go to a public school, make sure that you always know exactly what is being taught. Be one of those pain-in-the-neck parents, and don't—I repeat, don't—lean back and hand over your children's education to people you barely know. If you do, you are ignoring the sharks circling your kids. You shouldn't do that.

If you are fortunate enough to find a private school that you can afford—a school that upholds your values and has no sharks—that can certainly be a very good option. But make sure the curriculum is really what you expect. Some private schools that were excellent when you, or your parents, were young are now hopelessly secular; and a school is not Catholic just because it has that word carved above the entrance. Even if there are no sharks, there can be bad chemicals in that pool water, which is often the price of state funding.

When neither public schools nor private schools present a good option, more and more families today are turning to homeschooling. They're in good company. Let's take a look at how education happened at the Habsburg court.

Habsburg Homeschooling

The education of Habsburg archdukes and archduchesses most definitely resembles what we call homeschooling today. Indeed, for most of their 850 years on the European stage, the Habsburgs received their education at home (well, maybe "at palace").

There are important differences from today's situation, of course. For most of the Habsburg centuries, there were no general public schools. (Funnily enough, Empress Maria Theresia introduced this novel concept to her lands in the eighteenth century.) Also, emperors and empresses didn't educate their children themselves—they were working moms and dads, by definition—so they hired teachers to do the work, though in accordance with strict instruction from the parents. Finally, the Habsburg curriculum obviously reflected their position of privilege. The children were trained to be future rulers, soldiers, husbands and wives, priests and nuns (yes, those were the primary career options). As the mortality rate was high, all male descendants received more or less the same education, as there was always a chance a "spare" could become the heir. Even so, it is very interesting to see how they went about homeschooling. Some aspects of their programs seem quite familiar.

As early as Ferdinand in the sixteenth century, it was very important to learn many languages at home. It was common to read stories to children in languages not their own, so they would learn naturally and playfully. German, French, Italian, Czech, Polish, Hungarian, and Latin were frequently taught.

In addition to encouraging a diversity of languages, the Habsburgs wanted their children to learn a core set of values. Leopold I (who died in 1705) formulated it as piety, education, mercy, and loyalty. Riding and hunting were also important subjects to master, as was music. Leopold I himself composed music and played music together with his lovely wife, the famous Infanta Margherita (who is depicted in Velasquez paintings such as *Las Meninas* as well as in several portraits).

Maria Theresia (1740–1780) had very clear ideas about education and set them out clearly. Her sixteen children went to "home school" every day, all day, except on Sundays and holy days of obligation. (There were no free Saturdays for the archdukes.) Here's a list of the topics that her sons had to learn: religion, reading, writing, Latin, languages of the empire, history, geography, geology, military architecture, mathematics, music, dancing, sports, fencing, and riding; this was later complemented by metaphysics, logic, rhetoric, experimental physics, law studies, and physics. The empress's daughters learned some of this material as well, though not as extensively, as they were mostly expected to be wives and mothers.

Leopold, Grand Duke of Tuscany (who had sixteen children and later became Emperor Leopold II), was very clear about his principles of education. When they were three years old, his children began their first exercises in spelling. They were also brought in contact with different nurses who spoke different languages—German, French, and Italian—so they got used to hearing them all.

Whenever famous musicians, professors, or explorers passed through Florence, the future Leopold II (or Pietro Leopoldo, as the Italians called him) would invite them to the palazzo, where they would perform, give talks, or discuss their discoveries with the grand duke and his guests. But Leopold also saw to it that they would always visit the archducal home school. A famous German philosophy professor describes how he came into a room where three young archdukes were sitting in different corners, studying. One of them was working on Caesar's *Gallic War*; one of them was reading philosophy in a window niche. The professor quizzed them about what exactly they learned in philosophy. "Currently logic," they replied. Then he asked whether they had heard of a new, contemporary French philosopher. They answered, "We will read him next week."

Leopold II's son, Archduke Karl, wrote down his very detailed homeschooling plan from his childhood in Florence. In 1788, when the young archduke was about seven years old, his home curriculum looked like this.

7h Prayer, breakfast, spiritual reading
8h Riding or walking
9h History
10.15 Holy Mass (every day)
11h Math or French
13h Lunch and recreation
14.30 Latin
16 Recreation, music lessons twice a week
17h German or geography
18h Blessing and walk
18.30 Dinner and recreation
22.00 Sleeping

When Charles grew up, he did not simply adopt his parents' education plan for his own children. He stated, forty years later, "My sons go towards a different time, not the one I was raised in, and so they should be educated accordingly." The broad principles, however, remained the same: languages, soldiering, and sciences, supplemented by up-to-date material.

In the nineteenth century, the famous emperor Franz Joseph had, as a nine-year-old, thirty-seven hours of school per week, in addition to sports and riding. His native language was German, but at four years old, he spoke the Czech language better than his mother, Sophie, who tried to learn it at the same time he did.

But even in the twentieth century and after the end of the monarchy, Habsburg homeschooling continued. As a widow, Empress Zita traveled the world with her eight children in the 1930s. Here's a recollection of Archduke Otto of what his home curriculum looked like when he was the heir presumptive:

> I started at six in the morning. From six to eight I did my homework. Then, after half an hour's pause came the sessions with tutors, which lasted till midday. After lunch came more lessons until five o'clock, and then, until seven, I went on working by myself. My sister Adelheid studied with me from the beginning; the others joined in later one by one.

Not a bad way to learn. Not a bad way to grow up.

Homeschooling Experiences

The Habsburgs homeschooled their children over many centuries—and some (such as yours truly) still do to this day. Full disclaimer: like many families, we sometimes had children at "normal" schools and sometimes homeschooled. To a certain extent, it depended on the child. But in any case, I think we have quite a good understanding of the different systems.

The Habsburg history notwithstanding, many people are prejudiced against homeschooling and have in their heads weird images of secluded, gun-toting communities hiding in the forest, a bunch of weirdos shunning the world. This is nonsense on stilts. Homeschooling parents are extremely dedicated to their children's welfare and actively concerned about their future in the world. They've determined that they can manage their children's education more effectively than a one-size-fits-all institution. In some cases, however, they enroll their children in a homeschooling cooperative and follow its curriculum.

Practically speaking, homeschooled children become very self-motivated. A lot of home school consists of working on one's own and studying books that are part of a chosen curriculum. Modern technology also enables time in online classrooms with online teachers. Because these teachers can be selected from a global community, they are often far more expert in their chosen fields than the teachers at a local school ever could be. Furthermore, online classes are usually far smaller than the classes that most children experience. As for exams, they are taken in non-stress-inducing environments at home, supervised by parents (though ultimately verified by taking public exams, such as the SAT).

There are many advantages to this system and some disadvantages as well. The main advantage is that parents get to decide what their children learn. With homeschooling, there is no danger that your children will be indoctrinated or that crazy ideas (except your own) will be poured into your child's brain. It also allows you to give your child a truly Catholic education, which is not easy to find nowadays.

The level of education is typically far higher than comparable education in public or even private schools. You will immediately know where your children are excelling and where they are struggling—and you can instantly adjust your program accordingly. In a public school, children are often held back by the curriculum in some areas and pushed too fast in others. It can be quite a while before you realize this, and once you do, there is not much you can do about it anyway. One teacher who is responsible for dozens of children can do only so much.

As a result, homeschooled children, far from being forest-raised eccentrics, often seem far ahead of their peers. When I meet somebody who is truly impressive, I often find out that he or she was homeschooled. Among other things, I think this is because, in addition to the factual content of education, most homeschooling curricula take a special care in the human formation of children. A Catholic school will teach them the catechism and make them read the classics of spiritual literature. They learn early and take it to heart, and it makes it a big difference in the sort of people they grow up to become. I don't have to tell you that people who were homeschooled often make the best husbands and wives.

Another advantage of homeschooling is that families become independent with respect to location—at least as far as schooling, if not employment. This can be a great advantage if you want to live somewhere less expensive (perhaps in order to be able to afford to have many children). And the greatest perk for me? Children are at home all the time and can spend time with their siblings and parents—particularly if their parents are fortunate enough to be able to work remotely or, ideally, if their mothers have chosen to be stay-at-home moms.

Not being tied to an institutional schedule gives you enormous flexibility with your family time. You can go on vacation when you like (for example, when it is less expensive). If the children take their school stuff with them, you can even keep schooling as you travel.

Finally, your children will avoid the many bad influences that plague many schools, such as pornography, drugs, and harmful (sometimes dangerous) peer pressure.

Still, there are some disadvantages to homeschooling. While the most frequently heard concern—that children will become socially awkward—is overblown, there is always some danger of that. Especially when homeschooling alone, children without siblings can definitely become lonely.

If siblings are all homeschooled together, however, their social dynamics are very normal. In fact, it is much more natural, and less stressful, to have children of different ages together than to put children in large groups of peers of their exact age, every day for many years of their lives. Also, almost all homeschooling families arrange regular social activities with other children from the neighborhood or the parish.

Some parents may fear a social stigma from homeschooling. It's always a little hard to stand out in a crowd, to take charge of your own life. And some parents don't even want their children home all the time. Perhaps it interferes with the parents' work. Perhaps they don't feel the call to be their children's teachers or to sit beside their children all day long and correct their schoolwork. Fair enough. But if you feel otherwise, don't be overly influenced by the choices other people make for their own reasons.

Another thought: if you enroll your child in an online home school, he or she will learn with surprisingly little supervision. Online schools can be expensive, though usually less expensive than private schools. But it is a good hybrid method that can work for some families.

Finally, in many countries, homeschooling is made difficult—or impossible. The father of a homeschooling family I know works in Germany, but the family lives across the border in Austria, because homeschooling is illegal in Germany. In other places, homeschooling is highly regulated: you may use your wholesome curriculum, but your children must also take a yearly exam to show they have mastered the local, perhaps less wholesome, curriculum as well. These requirements can make the workload difficult to manage.

But if you conclude that homeschooling is the best way to educate your family, consider moving to a place that permits it. You are likely to find many similar families there and become part of a thriving, healthy community of like-minded souls.

Cell Phones, Computers, and Social Media

When it comes to children and phones and computers and social media, there is one principle and it is very easy: no.

No, for as long as possible.

Think of it this way: every month that your child has no phone or tablet at his or her disposal is a victory for that child's entire life. The earlier you give your children these devices—the earlier these tentacles of technology are plugged into their brains—the stronger the conditioning, the more intense the cravings they will have for this parallel world of sounds, pictures, and attractions.

This is not the place for an in-depth analysis of what cell phones have done to our world. But I believe that we are only beginning to understand the pernicious effects that these devices have had on the human psyche. Regardless of the dangerous content, the technology alone—which is getting better and better, and more and more entertaining by the minute—is addictive. I shudder to think about what it does to our minds, particularly young minds. Just believe me (and the many experts who are now saying this): the longer you can push back, the better for your children.

This can be difficult. As I said, children tend to do what they see their parents doing. If you spend every free minute on your computer or on phone apps, don't be surprised if your kids do that too. Unfortunately, we all know that living without phones today is practically impossible, so the key is moderation.

The moment children go to school, the pressure to have a phone becomes almost irresistible. Children who don't have a phone are socially excluded because they are not in the group chats. They are left out. They are alone.

But consider: the teasing and the bullying that happen in school all the time can now follow children home, if they have a phone.

So it is a conundrum.

Perhaps these three rules, which we have in our house, will be helpful.

1. No phones during lunch and dinner. Ideally, they should be in another room, so a real conversation can happen at the table.
2. In the evening, phones are charged in our common living room, not in our bedrooms. It is quite an idyllic scene, all those phones peacefully slumbering side by side. This is much easier to implement if the parents follow these rules, too. (We also try to stick to reading after a certain time of the evening. Ideally there should be no phones and no social media after a certain time—say, eight o'clock.)
3. Finally, no computers in the bedroom before a certain age. And this age should be pushed way, way up. The later, the better. You can have computers in the common rooms and use them in the public places. But not in your private room. Not until you are married (just kidding, but only a little).

To help manage the inevitable pushback, you can allow children to use your phone or the phone of a sibling for messages. This is ad hoc, so it doesn't create bad habits. But anything that puts any distance between a young child and a phone is helpful.

Before I conclude, I will acknowledge that a great blessing of the Internet and cell phone age—especially when your children are getting older and are no longer always at home—is to have a family group on one of the apps. We are very grateful to be able to be in constant contact with our children, even though they are spread over several countries. So technology has its place. But childhood has its place too. You get to experience it only once. Make sure your children don't miss it.

The Outdoors

You will remember that much of the Habsburg homeschooling curriculum involved outdoor activities. Children must get outside. Encourage them to collect mushrooms or rocks or plants; buy them books so they can identify the specimens they find. Teach them which plants you can eat and which can be used for teas or ointments. We are creatures made for the outdoors. Going out and enjoying adventures used to be one of the highlights of childhood. Don't let your children have an artificial childhood, glued to a screen.

Baking and Cooking

A lot of my time as a father was spent watching my daughters (and my one son) bake and cook. My wife, of course, passed on all the traditional family recipes. She has a special red book with handwritten recipes. One is for a kind of spice bread that must hearken back to the first half of the nineteenth century. It is a delicious secret that is handed down only in our family as part of our Christmas tradition. But there are many, many others. With five daughters around, the number of cakes, muffins, apple crumbles, and other sweets that emerged from our kitchen was nothing short of astonishing.

But take note: everyone needs to eat, and cooking is an important part of education. My son, who much preferred painting model airplanes, also learned his share of cooking.

The Facts of Life

This is a big topic. I don't really know where to squeeze it in. So I will include it here at the end of our discussion on education.

I have already said that values are the most important part of a child's education. This absolutely includes age-appropriate formation on marriage and family. If children go to school, they will very likely soon be confronted by pornographic images and very wrong ideas about sexuality. But even if they are homeschooled, our broader culture can be toxic to family life.

In some Catholic circles, parents are encouraged to teach children about the facts of life as early and in as detailed a way as possible. I agree that sexual education is a duty and right of parents. But I would be cautious about as "early" and "detailed." Rather, I would suggest being very sensitive to the different characters, sensitivities, and needs of your children.

When teaching about sexuality, it is important to determine first whether a child even *wants* to know more. Some are totally overwhelmed by these topics; some are bored and disinterested; some will have figured things out on their own; some will consider these topics terribly embarrassing, especially in conversations with their parents. Some would much prefer to learn certain things from their older siblings.

So what am I trying to say? One size definitely does not fit all here—definitely not. Be very careful about imposing too much information on your kids at too young an age, just so you can feel relieved about "having checked that part off." You might hurt them; they might even be angry with you. They might have reason to be. Here, as with so much of education, listening is terribly important.

And that's it! Now you have enough information to develop your own system of education, to pass on your values and your Faith and to weave the beautiful tapestry of your family. The rest is up to you—and to God.

And don't forget to pray too. Always.

5

The Role of Grandparents

Once your children begin looking for spouses of their own, you will enter a new phase of your life. The days when parents chose spouses for their children are long past. In fact, it is unusual—though wonderful—for parents to play a role in the choice of their children's spouses these days. (Some children still come to their parents for advice; sometimes they even listen.)

I can't say too much about being a grandparent yet. I am still a beginner. But I have a lot of family history, as you know. It guides me. Perhaps it can guide you too.

For example, Maria Theresia knew how important it was for her future daughters-in-law and sons-in-law to feel welcomed in the family. She did everything she could so they would feel at home. She regularly told her daughters-in-law, "I love you like my own daughter!"

Of course, the most famous "becoming a grandparent" story in our family is when Maria Theresia learned that her son Leopold had had his first son, the future Francis II. His birth ensured the survival of the Habsburg dynasty, which had been in doubt. When Maria Theresia—who hadn't left her apartments since the death of her husband—learned she had a grandson, she ran through Hofburg Castle and directly into her box in the Burgtheater, where a performance was in full swing. At the sudden appearance of the empress, the audience turned to her, eagerly. "Der Leopold hat an Buam!" she shouted, in her endearing Austrian dialect. "Leopold has a boy!" The entire room erupted in cheers.

But life has both joys and woes—and other Habsburg emperors suffered terribly for their grandchildren. Ferdinand I was devastated after his son Maximilian's wife lost a baby.

One Habsburg emperor who was a surprisingly tender grandfather (and great-grandfather) was Franz Joseph (with his huge white beard). Many saw this man as dry, duty-bound, and sometimes intimidating. But he had a very different side to him too.

We have private memories typed up by my own grandfather, Archduke Joseph Francis, in which he describes his encounters when he was young with his great-grandfather. Joseph describes the old emperor as having the gentlest blue eyes, a soft but clear voice, and slender, beautiful hands. Joseph loved his great-grandfather deeply and cherished the time he spent with him. Can you imagine this old soldier sitting with his grandchildren and great-grandchildren and playing with them?

> He often came into the royal garden in Budapest, where my sister, and my brother, and I were playing. We drew cities in the dirt and connected them with roads. The emperor sat down beside us, smiling, and helped us, with the tip of his walking-stick, to design these landscapes of our dreams.... I am writing this years later, sitting at a desk that once belonged to him, but as I write, I still feel his hand on my shoulder.

Grandparents can play a very important role in their grandchildren's lives. They can transmit values and family history and be very important role models in the Faith. I will always think about the role my grandfather Prince Löwenstein-Wertheim-Rosenberg played in my life. Though my parents taught me the Faith and world history at home, it was my grandfather who instilled in me a deep love for the Church, the papacy, and Church history.

Whenever we visited him, he went on a walk after lunch. He would always ask whether "someone" of his grandchildren wanted to come on that walk. We were all lazy, and a walk in the forest behind the house seemed a bit boring to us. Even so, I very often went along so I could spend time with him. I had the privilege of getting into long conversations with him.

He had played an important role in German Catholicism, and so he had a lot to say about the priests, bishops, and several popes with whom he had been friends. Through him I was first exposed to the "big picture" of Church and world. I doubt that I would have ever worked as a spokesman for a bishop or later become ambassador to the Holy See if it had not been for the influence of my grandfather.

Worldly achievements aside, grandparents are all called to live lives of prayer, praying especially for their grandchildren, and to be examples of piety. Here are a few details from Coulombe's biography that describe how Empress Zita spent her later years:

> Always pious, . . . Zita used the years in Zizers to become ever more devout. When driven past a church, she would cross herself; if walking, when passing a chapel, even with the door closed, she genuflected as much as her age would allow. In time, when this act of respect became too much for her physical strength, she never passed a church or chapel where the Blessed Sacrament was reserved without a bow and a moment of silence. Likewise, she spent long minutes preparing for the Most Holy Mass and even more time

recollecting herself in thanksgiving. Several witnesses speak of her spending approximately 15 to 30 minutes for preparation for Mass and 30 minutes of thanksgiving afterwards. According to one witness, "her assiduity at the monastic Offices was remarkable, as was her love of the Eucharist—in the Holy Sacrifice of the Mass and in the adoration of the Blessed Sacrament." As long as she was strong enough, she had THREE Holy Masses before breakfast and daily Rosary and devotions.

Most people don't know what a wonderful grandmother the empress was. At a conference in the United States, her granddaughter Maria-Anna Galitzine told of her first memory of meeting her grandmother, after a prolonged absence in another country, at the age of seven:

> I opened the door. There stood this old lady, very friendly but also intimidating, because she wore black as a widow. I accompanied her into the living room. She began talking to me. Soon, we were in deep conversation. She led me into a deeper understanding of the parts of the Holy Mass. She especially taught me the prayer for the departed souls during consecration. She spent a lot of time with us children.

Later, when Maria-Anna was fourteen and her mother suddenly died, Grandmother Zita soon appeared to help her son and his children. She had long conversations, certainly about the Faith, but also about all the other many topics her granddaughter wanted to know about. What an incredible gift for children bereft of their mother!

Maria-Anna said she remembered quizzing Zita endlessly about the different characters of Habsburg history whom she had met personally or heard about secondhand.

One final thought: when it comes to praying for your grandchildren, it is the most natural thing to do. My children regularly ask my mother—their grandmother—for her prayers, They also ask her advice for many big and small matters of heart and soul. They know they can trust her: she is a woman who practically lives with a rosary in her hand.

Our modern era would greatly benefit from grandparents who are present and play a role in the lives of their grandchildren. For all of us, and for our children, grandparents are a direct link to the past, to the whole world of yesteryear. We should treasure that mine of wonders. It fades, like a dream, all too fast.

6

Death in the Family

One of the best, most compelling reasons to have many children is that when you embark on the last part of your life's path, you will not be alone.

Perhaps this seems like a selfish reason. But it is not. God made us to be fruitful, and He made children to honor their parents. The fourth commandment says, "Honor thy father and thy mother," and this commandment was surely intended to include the years when parents are elderly and approaching death. Christ Himself quotes this commandment when He chides the Pharisees for substituting status-seeking donations to the temple for the duty owed to parents.

When you become old, your children have occasion to honor seriously one of the central commandments of God. This is good for their souls. Modern medicine has relieved many families of caring for ailing parents. As a result, "honoring" has started to mean little more than being nice to parents, perhaps visiting them from time to time, or hosting them at home. But when parents start ailing and getting weak and approaching death, this commandment becomes very important.

In my book *The Habsburg Way*, I wrote extensively about the good and holy way in which many members of the Habsburg family *prepared* for death and the way in which they organized their funerals. In this book, I want to speak about the way a family can *live* the death of a member. Once again, Habsburg history provides very beautiful examples of how things are "meant to be."

When you embark on your final grand voyage, you should be surrounded by your loved ones. This is how people died in the Habsburg family—surrounded by family. Whenever a family member died, whether it was the emperor or anyone else, it was the custom to call whoever was nearby. The dying Habsburg was then enveloped and cradled in prayers. I honestly cannot imagine a better way to go. Of course, you cannot choose your own death; you must humbly accept the death that God gives you. But being surrounded by family surely must be the best way, if it is given.

For example, the death, on January 18, 1761, of young Carl Joseph, one of Maria Theresia's sixteen children, occurred amid a smallpox epidemic. Carl Joseph was to have become the Grand Duke of Tuscany. But now he lay dying. He bore his suffering with great courage. A few days before his death, he received the last sacraments: Confession, Extreme Unction, and Communion. His family was present at that moment and in the days that followed: Emperor Franz Stephan, the archduke Joseph, and the archduchesses Isabella, Maria Anna, Maria Christina, and Maria Amalia. (I suppose the empress was absent because she was pregnant and was concerned about the risk of infection.)

Sixty-five years later, when Archduke Charles, victor over Napoleon, lay dying, his friend and confessor Provost Sedlaczek of Klosterneuburg Monastery administered the sacraments and remained with the archduke until he had breathed his last. But during Karl's last Holy Mass in the room, the entire imperial family was present and the weakened archduke took the time to bless every one of his children present. He himself said: "Death is the transition to

Him who loves us unendingly, and whose love alone can give us untarnished, never-ending happiness."

In 1780, when the great Maria Theresia felt her death nearing, she ordered that, after her death, Holy Masses should be said for her soul in thirty-two cities. While she was still mobile, she went down frequently into the Kapuzinergruft Crypt to pray by her deceased husband and her six children who had died, who all lay there. But when she was finally dying, her son Joseph (with whom her relations had always been strained) never moved an inch from her bedside. On November 26, the empress had difficulty breathing and immediately asked to be administered the Last Rites. Her agony was long and hard, and she was always conscious. Until her last breath, Joseph and several of her children stayed nearby and prayed.

Emperor Franz Joseph died in December 1916, surrounded by family, with his daughter Marie Valerie holding his crucifix near his lips so the weak emperor would be able to kiss it humbly.

And who could forget how the emperor Bl. Karl died: his wife was by his side, holding him in her arms as he called in his eldest son and heir, Otto, to let him witness "how an emperor dies."

My mother used to tell me how her own mother died. She was in a hospital bed, surrounded by all of her children. They prayed and even sang the song of Our Lady of Lourdes with her.

May the Lord grant each of us such a death. But may we also be prepared to accept whatever death is sent us. Some are very grim indeed.

For example, Empress Elisabeth, who was perhaps less devout than her husband, Franz Joseph, didn't have the comfort of a well-prepared death, surrounded by her family. She was knifed by an attacker in Geneva, in 1898, while boarding a ship, and expired shortly afterward in a room in the Hotel Beau Rivage.

But perhaps the years and years of prayers of her beloved daughter, Marie Valerie, for the soul of her mother were not in vain. I learned, while writing this book, that a priest was present while she lay dying in the hotel, and he gave her the absolution, while all present were kneeling and praying.

So please, please, be present when your parents are growing old. See to it that you are with them as much as you can be when they are in their final years, and months, and weeks, and days. Be with them, like the Habsburgs, if you like. This is what family is for. With God's help, I hope that, at my own death, I will be surrounded by my family, praying.

One more bit of encouragement, from my personal experience: it pays to be close to your parents, even if they seem unconscious or in a coma, even if you think they don't notice that you are there. When I was a boy, my mother caught meningoencephalitis and fell into a coma. For almost a week, she was unresponsive, though we often visited and sat by her bedside. When she (miraculously, I believe) recovered, she told us that when she seemed comatose, she was actually aware of what was going on most of the time and saw her surroundings quite well.

She said two things had given her hope and immense joy in the semidarkness of her condition: first, there was a crucifix in her room, and as long as she could see that, it was an enormous consolation; and second, whenever my father and my siblings and I were there, she knew that everything was good. From both of us, the same stream of love poured forth.

So spend time with your parents—even if the doctors say your parents "don't notice anything." You may be doing more good than you know.

Finally, remember that the duty of the family does not end with death. After the last moment comes, begin to pray for the deceased, to give him or her the best chance to go to Heaven—even if the priest says, at the funeral, that they are "with God now."

Make sure your parents get to Heaven swiftly by praying for them.

Afterword

The idea for this book was born at a Bl. Emperor Karl conference in Dallas in 2022. After the event, two girls came up to me and asked me whether it was even possible to have a spouse like Bl. Emperor Karl or a good marriage in today's sick world.

After reading this little book of mine, I hope that you see that the answer is a resounding yes. It's true that the world is in a very broken state. But it always has been, in different ways—and you can help to make it better.

Every family that lives according to the principles I have described helps heal the world and makes possible a better society. You can live your married life with your spouse according to God's plan, not according to the world's. You can raise your children according to your plan, and God's. Your home is your castle, in Habsburg terms; and the Lord is your Rock.

I have been blessed with the most wonderful wife in the world, with twenty-nine years of marriage, and with six children. Writing this book has given me a totally new appreciation of the miracle of family. I want the same blessings for you, and I promise to pray regularly for every reader of this book.

Go out there and build a wholesome family in a broken world.

A Habsburg Guide to Happiness

Before Marriage

Be faithful to your spouse before marriage.

Prepare for marriage years before you start dating.

Pray for your spouse, even before you meet him or her.

Chastity is the way to happiness.

Keep an open mind and consider whether you have a religious vocation.

Keep the list in mind.

Do not be intimate before marriage. Just don't. Trust me.

Talk about your faith when you are dating.

Talk about your ideas of family life.

Find out whether your potential spouse is open to life.

Building a Wholesome Family in a Broken World

Try to get to know your potential spouse's family.

Don't think you will change a potential spouse.

Be chaste.

Confess old relationships.

Learn about each other's characters.

Learn about each other's families.

Consider whether you are at peace when you are together.

Consider how you laugh with each other.

Do not have an intimate relationship yet!

Consider the practical matters of marriage.

Ask the opinion of your family.

When you are looking for a spouse, never lose hope.

Pray, pray, pray.

Become Catholic.

Be sober and strategic and cast your net wide.

When you are looking for a devout Catholic, look in churches.

But don't forget about Catholic dating sites.

Make a pilgrimage to a sanctuary of Bl. Karl.

Pray.

Listen to the voice of your heart.

Love, like faith, is ultimately a decision.

If you follow the truth, your feelings will follow you.

Relax. Pray. Decide. Jump.

During Your Engagement

Your engagement should not be a social media moment.

Warning signs may mean you are incompatible.

"Warning signs" may be diabolically inspired.

Don't worry about getting married young.

Do not move in together after you are engaged. *Be chaste.*

You are not married yet. Don't be afraid to keep discerning.

Don't be too scrupulous.

"Be cheerful, do good, and let the sparrows chirp."

Have a Catholic wedding.

Plan your liturgy and the event, but then let go.

Don't spend too much and cause financial stress.

Find a priest, ideally one who knows you well.

Ask him to speak about marriage, not just about you.

Ask God to grant that a couple will discern marriage at your wedding.

Have your wedding bands engraved.

When You're Married

If you are awed by what you have done, pray together.

Keep working on your love and relationship.

Don't let the sun set on a conflict.

Pray. And help each other get to Heaven.

Have children, many children.

Don't use contraception.

A large family is the greatest gift you can give to your children.

If you have trouble having children, don't lose hope.

If you can't have children, trust that
God has another plan for you.

God may want you to be a foster parent or adopt.

Children make you closer as a couple.

When Children Come Along

Mothers should be at home, if at all possible.

Spend lots of time with your children.

Embrace with special love children with special needs.

When you are expecting a child, talk to God.

Pray as a couple.

Pray on your own.

Thank God for your children.

Have others **pray** for you.

Baptize your children as soon as you can.

Name your children after saints.

Get as much sleep as you can manage.

Summon up your spirit of adventure.

Look at your baby, and marvel at how your baby looks at you.

Ask your friends, or family, for advice.

Resume going to Mass as soon as you can.

Keep romance alive in your marriage.

In Educating Your Children

Share the things you love with your children.

Think carefully about your children's education.

Keep their moral education at the forefront.

Children will do what they see you do, including with respect to faith.

Fathers are the key to passing on the Faith.

Say regular **prayers**, in the morning and in the evening.

Find a church that brings you closer to God.

Make Confession part of your children's religious life.

Make pilgrimages.

Include children in family chores as early as possible.

Spend time with your children.

Show your children that you love them.

Share the things you love with your children.

Read to your children.

Pass on your family's traditions and rituals.

Encourage your children to perform plays and give concerts.

Make sure you know what your children are being taught.

Consider homeschooling your children.

Say no to cell phones and computers for as long as possible.

Spend time outdoors.

Teach your children to bake and cook.

Talk to your children about sexuality when they are ready.

As Your Parents Age

Grandparents play an important role
in their grandchildren's lives.

Care for your parents when they get old.

The duty of family does not end with death.
Pray for their souls.

About the Author

Eduard Habsburg is Hungary's ambassador to the Holy See and the Sovereign Order of Malta. His family reigned in Austria, Hungary, Germany, and Spain (and quite a few other places). Also known as Archduke Eduard of Austria, he is a diplomat and social media personality. Eduard and his wife, Baroness Maria Theresia von Gudenus, have six children. Eduard is the author of several books, including the children's book *Dubbie: The Double-Headed Eagle*; volumes on Thomas Aquinas, James Bond, and Harry Potter; novels; and screenplays.

Sophia Institute

Sophia Institute is a nonprofit institution that seeks to nurture the spiritual, moral, and cultural life of souls and to spread the gospel of Christ in conformity with the authentic teachings of the Roman Catholic Church.

Sophia Institute Press fulfills this mission by offering translations, reprints, and new publications that afford readers a rich source of the enduring wisdom of mankind.

Sophia Institute also operates the popular online resource CatholicExchange.com. *Catholic Exchange* provides world news from a Catholic perspective as well as daily devotionals and articles that will help readers to grow in holiness and live a life consistent with the teachings of the Church.

In 2013, Sophia Institute launched Sophia Teachers to renew and rebuild Catholic culture through service to Catholic education. With the goal of nurturing the spiritual, moral, and cultural life of souls, and an abiding respect for the role and work of teachers, we strive to provide materials and programs that are at once enlightening to the mind and ennobling to the heart; faithful and complete, as well as useful and practical.

Sophia Institute gratefully recognizes the Solidarity Association for preserving and encouraging the growth of our apostolate over the course of many years. Without their generous and timely support, this book would not be in your hands.

www.SophiaInstitute.com
www.CatholicExchange.com
www.SophiaTeachers.org

Sophia Institute Press is a registered trademark of Sophia Institute.
Sophia Institute is a tax-exempt institution as defined by the Internal Revenue Code, Section 501(c)(3). Tax ID 22-2548708.